CHARLES VANCE

Foundations of Jython Programming

A Beginners guide to scripting in Inductive Automation's Ignition

First edition

This book was professionally typeset on Reedsy.
Find out more at reedsy.com

Contents

Chapter 01: Introduction to Jython

1.1 What is Jython in the Context of Ignition?

Jython is a Python 2.7 implementation that runs within the Java-based architecture of Ignition by Inductive Automation. It powers all scripting inside the platform—from expression bindings and tag events to gateway scripts and Vision/Perspective actions. In Ignition, you don't need to install Jython separately—it's already embedded, giving you the full flexibility of Python 2 scripting with seamless access to Ignition's Java-based APIs. Understanding Jython is key to unlocking advanced logic, automation, and customization in your SCADA and HMI projects.

1.2 Setting Up Your Ignition Scripting Environment

Step-by-Step: Setting Up Your Ignition Scripting Environment

Step 1: Download and Install Ignition

- Go to the official Inductive Automation website:
- https://inductiveautomation.com
- Click on "Download Ignition".
- Choose the version compatible with your operating system (Windows, macOS, or Linux).
- Run the installer and follow the on-screen instructions to install Ignition.

Step 2: Launch the Ignition Gateway

- After installation, the Ignition Gateway should start automatically.
- If not, open your browser and go to http://localhost:8088 to access the Gateway homepage.
- Follow the setup wizard to configure your initial settings (username, password, project name).

Step 3: Open the Designer

- From the Gateway homepage, click "Launch Designer".
- Download the Designer Launcher if prompted.
- Use the launcher to open the Ignition Designer.

- Log in using the credentials you set up during installation.
- Open or create a new project.

Step 4: Open the Script Console

- Inside the Designer, go to the Tools menu.
- Select Script Console.
- This is your interactive Jython environment. You can write and run Jython 2.7 scripts here in real-time.

Step 5: Explore Scripting Areas in Ignition

The **Script Console** in the Ignition Designer serves as your built-in scripting IDE, perfect for experimenting with Jython in a safe, isolated environment. Here's how to make the most of it while learning:

- **Write and test code interactively**: Use the console to type and run Jython scripts in real time. It's ideal for learning syntax, testing logic, and getting instant feedback without affecting your live project.
- **Explore Ignition's scripting functions**: Try out system functions like system.tag.readBlocking(), system.gui.messageBox(), or system.date.now() to understand how Ignition interacts with tags, GUI, and system data.
- **Prototype before deploying**: Develop snippets in the console, then transfer working code into more permanent scripting locations like Tag Events or Component Events.
- **Access real project context**: The console has access to your project's scope, including tags, components, and data—so you can experiment using real objects.

Once you're comfortable, start moving your scripts into the following areas:

- **Tag Events** – Automate behavior based on tag value changes.

3

- **Component Events** – Add interactivity to buttons, tables, and charts.
- **Gateway Event Scripts** – Run scripts on the server, such as startup tasks or tag change listeners.
- **Named Scripts** – Organize reusable functions into script modules.
- By using the Script Console as your Jython playground, you can rapidly build confidence and skill before applying code to critical components.

Step 6: No Extra Setup Needed

- No separate installation of Jython or Java is required—Ignition includes everything out of the box.
- You're now ready to begin scripting and learning Jython within the Ignition platform.

1.3 How Jython in Ignition Differs from Traditional Python

Feature	Jython in Ignition	Traditional Python (CPython)
Version	Python 2.7 only	Python 2.x or 3.x
Interpreter Base	Java-based	C-based
Java Integration	Full access to Java and Ignition APIs	No built-in Java access
Performance	Optimized for Java environments	Generally faster for pure Python
Native Libraries	No C extension support (e.g., NumPy)	Supports C-based modules
Use Case	Industrial SCADA scripting	General-purpose Python development

Chapter 02: Variables and Data Types

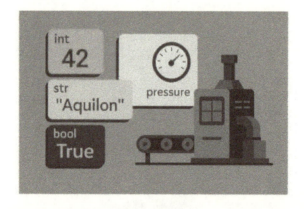

In Ignition scripting, variables are used to store and manipulate data during automation tasks. Jython supports standard data types such as integers, floats, strings, and booleans, along with complex types like lists, tuples, dictionaries, and datasets. Understanding how to declare and use variables is essential for scripting logic, processing tag values, handling user input, and interacting with components. Ignition also uses datasets and PyDatasets to represent tables of data—requiring conversion for Python-style access using system.dataset.toPyDataSet(). Mastering data types allows developers to write clear, efficient, and accurate automation scripts.

2.1 Declaring and Using Variables in Scripts

This example demonstrates how to declare and use **variables** and **basic data types** in Ignition scripting with Jython:

```
temperature = system.tag.readBlocking(
            "[Site A]Sensors/Sensor 1/Temperature"
            )[0].value
operatorName = "Charles"
isRunning = True

print temperature
print operatorName
print isRunning
```

temperature:

This variable stores the value of a tag read from the Ignition system.

- system.tag.readBlocking() reads the value of the tag at "[Site A]Sensors/Sensor 1/Temperature" synchronously.
- [0].value accesses the first (and only) result and gets its value.
- The data type is likely a float or int, depending on how the tag is configured.

operatorName:

A **string variable** storing the name "Charles". This might be used for logging, display, or authentication logic.

isRunning:

A **boolean variable** set to True, typically used in control logic to check if a machine or process is active.

print statements:

These display the current values of the variables in the console, which is useful for debugging or feedback during script execution.

the figure below is how the statement appears in the ignition Script Console and what the result looks like in the right execution pane.

Script Console

Multiline Buffer

```
 1  temperature = system.tag.readBlocking(
 2                              "[Site A]Sensors/Sensor 1/Temperature"
 3                              )[0].value
 4  operatorName = "Charles"
 5  isRunning = True
 6
 7  print temperature
 8  print operatorName
 9  print isRunning
10
11
12
```

Interactive Interpreter

```
Jython 2.7.3, executing locally in the Designer.
Press (Ctrl + Space) to activate autocompletion.
>>>
94.7729981572
Charles
True
>>>
```

2.2 Numeric Types in Automation Contexts

Jython supports integers, floats, and long numbers—all useful in industrial calculations like scaling sensor data or converting units. Example:

```
flowRate = 12.5
setpoint = 100
remaining = setpoint - flowRate

print remaining
```

In automation systems, numeric values—especially **floats** and **integers**—are used constantly for monitoring, control, and decision-making. This script shows a basic example of **flow control logic** using numeric types:

- flowRate = 12.5 → a **float** value representing the **current process flow**, such as gallons per minute.
- setpoint = 100 → an **integer** value indicating the **target total** or **desired quantity**, such as gallons to dispense.
- remaining = setpoint - flowRate → this line calculates how much flow still needs to occur to reach the setpoint.

The subtraction operation between a float and an int results in a float:

- 100 – 12.5 = 87.5, which is stored in remaining.

This kind of calculation is typical in batching, filling systems, or any process that tracks material flow toward a target. The result (remaining) might be used to determine how long to keep a valve open or when to trigger the next stage of a sequence.

Here is what the operation looks like in the Ignition Script Console. (I'm not going to show you this every time I promise.)

Script Console

Multiline Buffer

```
1  flowRate = 12.5
2  setpoint = 100
3  remaining = setpoint - flowRate
4
5  print remaining
6
```

Interactive Interpreter

```
Jython 2.7.3, executing locally in the Designer.
Press (Ctrl + Space) to activate autocompletion.
>>>
>>>
87.5
>>>
```

2.3 Strings for Messages, Tags, and Logs

Strings are essential in Ignition scripting for handling text-based information such as operator messages, tag paths, and log entries. They allow dynamic construction of tag references, customized user feedback, and detailed logging for diagnostics. Strings can be combined using concatenation (+), formatted with .format() or f-strings, and processed using methods like .lower(), .strip(), or .replace(). Mastery of strings enables flexible, readable, and maintainable automation scripts that clearly communicate system behavior and state.

This script demonstrates how to use **strings** in Ignition scripting to build clear, human-readable messages for interfaces, logs, or alarms:

```
name = "Pump"
status = "Running"
fullStatus = name + " is " + status

print FullStatus
```

name = "Pump" A string variable storing the name of the device or component.

- status = "Running"

Another string storing the current operational state of the device.

- fullStatus = name + " is " + status

This line concatenates the three strings into one complete message:

- "Pump is Running"

This pattern is widely used in automation to generate **status messages**, **system logs**, or **UI labels**. For example:

- On a dashboard label: Pump is Running
- In a log file: Compressor is Faulted
- As an alarm description: Valve is Open

In Ignition, strings are crucial for system logs, the new line of code uses Ignition's built-in logging system to print a message tagged with a custom logger name:

```
name = "Pump"
status = "Running"
fullStatus = name + " is " + status

system.util.getLogger("MyLogger").info("Status: " + fullStatus)
```

If you run this line from the **Script Console** inside the **Ignition Designer**, the message will **only appear in the Output Console** at the bottom of the Designer.

Output Console

```
18:06:08.073 [SwingWorker-pool-1-thread-10] INFO MyLogger -- Status: Pump is Running
```

It **will not appear** in the **Gateway Logs** or **Vision Client Logs**, because the Script Console runs in the Designer's local scope.

To view log messages in the Gateway Logs or Client Logs, you must run the script from:

- A **Vision component event** (like a button click)
- A **Perspective event**
- A **Gateway Timer Script**
- A **Tag Change script**
- Or another runtime context

String manipulation like this helps make your scripts more informative, enabling real-time status reporting, alarm messages, or audit logs that operators and technicians can easily understand.

2.4 Type Conversion in Ignition Scripts

Type conversion in Ignition scripting is the process of changing a value from one data type to another, such as converting a string to a number or a float to an integer. This is often necessary when working with tag values, user input, or database data that may not be in the expected format. Ignition uses built-in Python functions like int(), float(), and str() to perform conversions. Proper type conversion ensures accurate calculations, prevents runtime errors, and enables seamless interaction between tags, components, and scripts in automation workflows.

This script demonstrates **type conversion also known as "type casting"**, an essential practice in Ignition scripting when handling tag data, user input, or string-based configuration:

```
valueStr = str(42) # "42"
valueInt = int("10") # 10
valueFloat = float("3.14") # 3.14
```

valueStr = str(42)

- Converts the integer 42 into a string:
- Result: "42"
- Used when you want to display numeric values in a label, message, or log.

valueInt = int("10")

- Converts the string "10" into an integer:
- Result: 10
- Useful when reading numeric input from a text field or tag that stores numbers as strings.

valueFloat = float("3.14")

- Converts the string "3.14" into a floating-point number:
- Result: 3.14
- Often used when performing math with decimal values that come from string sources.

In Ignition, tag values, user input, and query results often need to be converted before they can be used in calculations or displayed. For example:

- *A numeric string from a text field must be converted to an int before comparison.*
- *A sensor value might need to be converted to str for logging.*

· *A database value might come in as a string and need conversion to float for arithmetic.*

Proper use of str(), int(), and float() ensures your automation scripts work safely and correctly.

2.5 Best Practices for Variable Use in Ignition

In Ignition scripting, using variables effectively improves script readability, maintainability, and reliability. Use clear, descriptive variable names that reflect their purpose, such as flowRate or isAlarmActive. Always initialize variables before use, and keep scopes limited to where they're needed. When working with tag values or user input, apply proper type conversion (int(), float(), str()) to avoid errors. Organize logic by grouping related variables, avoid reusing names unintentionally, and use comments to clarify purpose. Following these practices results in clean, consistent, and automation-ready code:

· **Name clearly**: Use names like motorStatus, alarmCode, or userID.
· **Avoid hardcoding**: Pull values from tags or components.
· **Use constants for fixed values**: Keep them at the top of the script.
· **Test in Script Console**: Always validate logic in small steps.
· **Comment your logic**: Especially in Gateway or Tag Event Scripts.

Clean, purposeful variable use leads to reliable automation code that's easier to debug and maintain.

Sample Exercises

Exercise 1: Create and Print Variables

- **Objective**: Declare variables of different data types and print their values.
- **Steps** (run in the Script Console):

```
deviceName = "Pump A"
temperature = 78.6
isRunning = True
runtimeHours = 142

print deviceName
print temperature
print isRunning
print runtimeHours
```

What You Learn: How to declare and use str, float, bool, and int types.

Exercise 2: Read a Tag Value into a Variable

- **Objective**: Assign a tag value to a variable and print it.
- **Create a tag:** [default]Boiler/Pressure with a numeric value.
- **Script**:

```
amps = system.tag.readBlocking(["[Site A]Machine 1/Amps"])[0].value
print "Machine 1 Amps:", amps
```

Make sure your project has this tagpath or select one of your own.

Tip: Copy/Paste the tagpath directly from the tag, be sure to match the syntax when you paste in the tagpath. "[Site A]Machine 1/Amps" (or the one you choose)

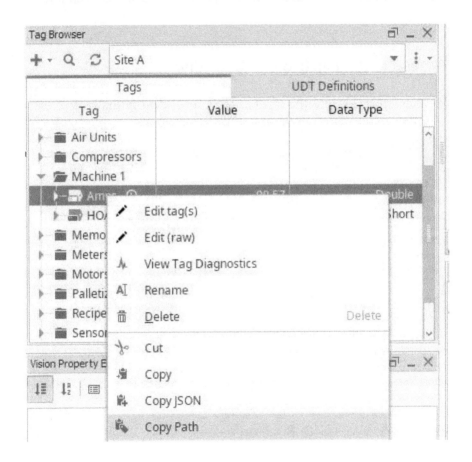

Exercise 3: Type Conversion and Concatenation

- **Objective**: Convert a number to a string and build a readable message.
- **Script**:

```
rpm = 1350
message = "Current RPM: " + str(rpm)
print message
```

What You Learn: How to convert between data types using str() and concatenate strings.

Exercise 4: Use type() to Check Data Types

- **Objective**: Explore the type() function to identify the type of each variable.
- **Script**:

```
name = "Sensor A"
level = 24.5
active = False

print type(name)
print type(level)
print type(active)
```

What You Learn: How to inspect data types dynamically in the Script Console.

Exercise 5: Work with Boolean Values

- **Objective**: Write a script that checks a boolean and responds accordingly.
- Create a Memory Tag [default]Pump/Running (Boolean).
- **Script**:

```
IsRunning = system.tag.readBlocking(["[Site A]Pump/Running"])[0].value
if IsRunning:
    print "Pump is running."
else:
    print "Pump is stopped."
```

Manipulate the tag by setting it true then false and execute the script in the Script Console each time.

What You Learn: How to use boolean values to control logic flow.

3

Chapter 03: Operators and Expressions

Operators and expressions in Ignition scripting allow you to perform calculations, make comparisons, and build logic for automation tasks. Arithmetic, comparison, logical, and assignment operators are used to evaluate conditions, process data, and control system behavior. Expressions combine values, variables, and operators into meaningful instructions that drive tag writes, component updates, and decision-making. Understanding how to construct and use expressions ensures precise, readable, and effective scripting for real-time industrial control.

3.1 Arithmetic Operators for Industrial Logic

Arithmetic operators like +, -, *, /, and % are used in Ignition scripting to perform essential calculations in industrial automation. This example shows how to use **arithmetic operators** in an automation context to calculate total production output:

```
# Example: Calculate total production
unitsPerMinute = 45
minutes = 60
totalUnits = unitsPerMinute * minutes  # 2700

print totalUnits
```

unitsPerMinute = 45

- This variable stores the production rate—how many units the system produces per minute (e.g., parts, bottles, or packages).

minutes = 60

- This represents the total run time of the process in minutes (1 hour in this case).

totalUnits = unitsPerMinute * minutes

- The multiplication operator * calculates how many units were produced in 60 minutes:
- 45 * 60 = 2700

totalUnits equals 2700, meaning 2,700 units were produced during the hour.

- Supported operators: +, -, *, /, %, ** (exponent), // (floor division)
- Try your formulas in the Script Console before embedding them into tag event or expression logic.

This type of calculation is commonly used in:

- *OEE (Overall Equipment Effectiveness) reporting*
- *Shift production summaries*
- *Batch process tracking*
- *Efficiency analysis*

Simple arithmetic like this forms the basis of more advanced scripting logic in Ignition.

3.2 Comparison Operators for Conditions

This script demonstrates a **basic conditional statement** using an if clause to trigger an action when a specific condition is met—common in automation alarm logic:

```
temperature = 85
If temperature > 80:
    system.gui.messageBox("High Temp Alarm!")
```

temperature = 85

This assigns a numeric value (85) to the variable temperature, simulating a reading from a sensor or tag.

if temperature > 80:

This is a conditional check:

- It evaluates whether the current temperature exceeds 80. Since 85 > 80 is true, the code inside the block will run.

system.gui.messageBox("High Temp Alarm!")

This displays a popup message to the user with the text "High Temp Alarm!".

- This is typically used in **Vision Clients** to alert operators of a condition that needs attention.

Operators include: ==, !=, >, <, >=, <=

- *Use these in tag change scripts or to control visibility in Vision/Perspective.*

3.3 Logical Operators for Complex Checks

Logical operators allow you to combine multiple conditions in a single expression, making your scripts more powerful and flexible for real-world automation logic.

Here's a a **conditional logic example** using two real-world Ignition tags:

- [Site A]Compressors/Compressor 1/motorAmps
- [Site A]Compressors/Compressor 2/motorAmps.

```
amps1 = system.tag.readBlocking(
                ["[Site A]Compressors/Compressor 1/motorAmps"]
                    )[0].value
amps2 = system.tag.readBlocking(
                ["[Site A]Compressors/Compressor 2/motorAmps"]
                    )[0].value

If amps1 > 150 and amps2 > 150:
    system.tag.writeBlocking(
                ["[Site A]Alarms/HighAmpsBothCompressors"]
                , [True])
```

amps1 and amps2:

These read the current motor amps from both compressors.

if amps1 > 150 and amps2 > 150:

- Uses the and logical operator to check if both compressors are drawing more than 150 amps.

If the condition is met, it triggers an alarm by

- writing True to the [Site A]Alarms/HighAmpsBothCompressors tag.

Logical operators allow you to combine multiple conditions in a single expression, making your scripts more powerful and flexible for real-world automation logic. In Ignition, the three main logical operators are:

- *and – Returns True only if all conditions are true.*
- *Example: if amps1 > 100 and amps2 > 100: triggers logic only when both conditions are met.*
- *or – Returns True if at least one condition is true.*
- *Example: if temp > 90 or pressure > 120: will act if either threshold is exceeded.*
- *not – Reverses the condition's result.*
- *Example: if not isRunning: checks if something is not currently active.*

These operators are essential when building alarm logic, safety checks, startup conditions, and any process that depends on multiple input states. They help create clean, readable, and reliable automation scripts that respond to complex system behaviors.

3.4 Assignment and Compound Operators

This script demonstrates how to use **augmented assignment operators** (+=, *=) to update a variable's value efficiently—something very common in loop counters, totals, or process calculations in Ignition scripting.

```
count = 0
print count
count += 5   # same as count = count + 5
print count
count *= 2   # count becomes 10
print count
```

count = 0

- Initializes the variable count to zero. This is often the starting point for counters or accumulators.

print count

- Outputs: 0

count += 5

- Adds 5 to the current value of count.
- It's shorthand for: count = count + 5
- Now, count is 5.

print count

- Outputs: 5

count *= 2

- Multiplies the current value of count by 2.
- Now, count becomes 10.

print count

- Outputs: 10

You might use this logic to:

- *Tally the number of completed batches.*
- *Accumulate flow totals.*
- *Adjust a control parameter based on feedback.*

Using augmented assignment operators like +=, -=, *=, and /= helps keep code clean, readable, and efficient—especially when modifying variables inside loops or condition-based logic in Ignition.

3.5 Expressions in Ignition Scripting

This script demonstrates a simple **unit conversion** from Celsius to Fahrenheit using arithmetic operations—common in industrial environments where temperature sensors report in one scale and displays or logic require another.

```
tempC = 30
tempF = tempC * 9.0 / 5 + 32
print tempF
```

tempC = 30

- Assigns 30 to tempC, representing a temperature of **30 degrees Celsius**.

tempF = tempC * 9.0 / 5 + 32

- Converts the Celsius value to Fahrenheit using the standard formula:

F = C × 9/5 + 32

- So:
- tempF = 30 * 9.0 / 5 + 32 = 86.0

print tempF

- Outputs: 86.0

In Vision or Perspective bindings, you'll also use **Expression Language**, but inside scripts, **Jython expressions** are more flexible and powerful.

Use expressions to:

- Scale analog values
- Format display text
- Enable conditional logic
- Control alarms or interlocks

Temperature sensors might output data in Celsius, but operators or reports may require Fahrenheit. This kind of conversion logic can be used in:

- *Tag expression bindings*
- *Script transforms in Perspective*
- *Report calculations*
- *Alarming conditions based on converted values*

By handling unit conversions directly in your script, you ensure consistency and clarity across the system.

Sample Exercises

Exercise 1: Perform Arithmetic Operations

Objective: Use arithmetic operators with numeric tag values.

  Setup: Create two memory tags:

- [Site A]Motors/Motor 1/Speed
- [Site A]Motors/Motor 1/Speed

Script:

```
s1 = system.tag.readBlocking(["[Site A]Motors/Motor 1/Speed"])[0].value
print "Motor 1 Speed:", s1
s2 = system.tag.readBlocking(["[Site A]Motors/Motor 2/Speed"])[0].value
print "Motor 2 Speed:", s2
averageSpeed = (s1 + s2) / 2
print "Average Speed:", averageSpeed
```

What You Learn: How to apply +, /, and parentheses to evaluate expressions.

Exercise 2: Use Comparison Operators

Objective: Compare tag values and take action.

Script:

```
temp = 87
if temp > 90:
   print "Overheating!"
elif temp == 90:
   print "At limit."
else:
   print "Temperature normal."
```

What You Learn: How to use >, ==, and < to evaluate conditions.

Exercise 3: Combine Logical Operators

Objective: Use and, or, and not in a multi-condition check.

Setup: Create tags:

- [Site A]Tank/Tank1/Level = 75
- [Site A]Tank/Tank1/ValveOpen = False

Script:

```
level = system.tag.readBlocking(["[Site A]Tank/Tank1/Level"])[0].value
valve = system.tag.readBlocking(["[Site A]Tank/Tank1/ValveOpen"])[0].value

if level > 70 and not valve:
   print "Warning: Tank full but valve is closed!"
else:
   print "Tank Normal"
```

What You Learn: How to use and, or, and not to create logical expressions.

Exercise 4: Use Compound Assignment Operators

Objective: Simplify math with assignment operators.

Script:

```
runtime = 100
print "Initialize runtime:",runtime
runtime += 20
print "Increment runtime:",runtime
runtime *= 2
print "Adjusted runtime:", runtime
```

What You Learn: How to use +=, -=, *=, /= for shorthand calculations.

Exercise: Calculate Tank Fill Percentage

Objective:

· Calculate how full a tank is based on the current level and maximum capacity using arithmetic operators.

Script :

```
# Tank fill percentage calculation
currentLevel = 3200   # in gallons
tankCapacity = 5000   # in gallons

fillPercent = (float(currentLevel) / tankCapacity) * 100

print "Tank Fill Percentage:", round(fillPercent, 2), "%"
```

What You Learn:

- *How to apply arithmetic operators to solve real-world problems*
- *How to convert values to float for accurate division*
- *How to round and format output for operator readability*

This is a foundational example used in many automation systems for monitoring and control.

4

Chapter 04: Control Flow – Conditional Logic

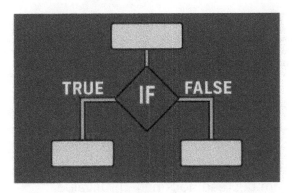

Conditional logic allows Ignition scripts to make decisions based on data or system states using if, elif, and else statements. These structures evaluate conditions and execute code only when specific criteria are met. Logical operators like and, or, and not are used to build more complex conditions. Conditional logic is essential for tasks such as triggering alarms, responding to sensor values, or controlling equipment based on multiple inputs. It enables dynamic, responsive automation by directing script behavior based on real-time conditions.

4.1 Using if Statements to Control Logic

Conditional statements let your script make decisions. In Ignition, they're used for:

- Tag change responses
- Alarm triggers
- Interface actions

This script demonstrates how to use **conditional logic** in Ignition to monitor a tag value and trigger a message when a threshold is exceeded.

Script

```
level = system.tag.readBlocking(["[Site A]Tank/Tank1/Level"])[0].value
print level
if level > 32:
    system.gui.messageBox("Tank Level High")
```

level = system.tag.readBlocking([...])[0].value

- Reads the current value of the tag [Site A]Tank/Tank1/Level. This is typically a numeric value representing the liquid level in a tank. The .value extracts the actual data from the returned tag object.

print level

- Outputs the current level to the Designer's Output Console (if run from the Script Console) or to system logs (if redirected). Useful for debugging or verification.

if level > 32:

- A conditional statement that checks if the tank level exceeds 32. If true, the next line executes.

system.gui.messageBox("Tank Level High")

- Displays a popup alert in the **Vision Client** warning the operator that the tank level is too high.

This logic is typical for monitoring process conditions like tank levels, temperatures, pressures, or speeds. When thresholds are crossed, scripts like this can trigger visual alerts, write alarm tags, or initiate control logic. It provides a responsive and readable way to implement real-time checks inside Ignition.

4.2 Adding else and elif for Flexible Logic

This script demonstrates how to use **conditional logic** to evaluate a numeric value and assign a status label based on defined thresholds. It simulates real-world decision-making logic used in automation systems for monitoring and alerting. It uses **conditional logic** to classify a numeric value (in this case, a level) into one of three categories: "Critical High", "High", or "Normal". It then prints the assigned alert.

Script

```
level = 91

if level > 90:
    alert = "Critical High"
elif level > 80:
    alert = "High"
else:
    alert = "Normal"

print alert
```

level = 91

- This sets the current reading (e.g., tank level) to 91.

First Condition – if level > 90:

- Since 91 is greater than 90, this condition evaluates to **True**.
- The script sets alert = "Critical High" and skips the rest of the conditional checks.

Second Condition – elif level > 80:

- This is **not evaluated** because the first condition was already met.

Final Case – else:

- This runs **only if** none of the previous conditions are true. In this case, it is skipped.

Output – print alert

· Prints: Critical High

Level Value	Condition Met	Alert
91+	`level > 90`	"Critical High"
81–90	`level > 80` (but ≤ 90)	"High"
80 or less	neither condition is True	"Normal"

This structure is commonly used for:

- *Triggering different levels of alarms*
- *Updating color-coded status indicators*
- *Sending alerts or warnings based on process thresholds*

It ensures the system reacts appropriately based on severity, with only one outcome selected per evaluation cycle.

4.3 Nesting Conditions in Scripts

Nesting means putting one condition **inside** another. In scripting, this helps you control the flow of your program more carefully. You can check one thing *first*, and *then* check something else only if the first thing is true.

Script

```
machineStatus = "Running"
temperature = 90
If machineStatus == "Running":
  if temperature > 100:
    system.tag.writeBlocking([["[Site A]Machine 1/Alarms"], [True])

value = system.tag.readBlocking([["[Site A]Machine 1/Alarms"])[0].value
print value
```

machineStatus = "Running"

- This sets a variable named machineStatus to the text "Running". It's like saying, "The machine is currently on."
- temperature = 90
- This sets a variable named temperature to the number 90. Imagine it's reading the machine's temperature.

if machineStatus == "Running":

- This is the **first condition**. It checks if the machine is running. If it is, the code inside this block will run.
- If it's *not* running, nothing inside this block will happen.

if temperature > 100:

- This is a **nested condition**. It's inside the first one.
- It checks if the temperature is greater than 100. But it only checks this **if the machine is running**.

system.tag.writeBlocking(["[Site A]Machine 1/Alarms"], [True])

- If both conditions are true (the machine is running *and* the temperature is too high), this line turns on the alarm by writing True to the alarm tag.

value = system.tag.readBlocking(["[Site A]Machine 1/Alarms"])[0].value

- This reads the current value of the alarm tag—whether it's on (True) or off (False)—and stores it in a variable called value.

print value

- *Nesting allows you to check one condition inside another.*
- *This code only triggers the alarm if the machine is running and the temperature is too high.*
- *It's a smart way to make your script behave logically and avoid unnecessary actions.*

Keep nesting clear and readable. Avoid too many levels—extract logic into functions when possible.

4.4 Truthy and Falsy Values in Ignition

In Python (and Ignition scripting), values are not just *True* or *False*—they can be **truthy** or **falsy**. This means that some values will automatically behave like True, and others like False, even if they aren't literally True or False.

In Jython, these values are treated as False in conditions:

- 0, 0.0
- ' ' (empty string)
- [], {}, None

When you write an if statement, Python checks whether the value is **truthy** or **falsy**.

- **Truthy** means "Python considers this value to be true."
- **Falsy** means "Python considers this value to be false."

Script

```
operator = ''
if not operator:
    system.gui.messageBox("No operator logged in.")
```

Here, operator is an **empty string**, which is a **falsy** value. So not operator becomes True, and the message box shows up.

When working with tag values, user inputs, or sensor readings in Ignition, you'll often use conditions like if not value: to catch things like:

- *Empty fields*
- *Zero values*
- *Missing data*

Using truthy and falsy logic helps you simplify your code and handle unexpected conditions gracefully

4.5 Common Conditional Use Cases in Ignition

- **Alarm logic:** Trigger alarms based on thresholds or combined conditions.
- **Visibility rules:** Show/hide components based on user roles or tag states.
- **Process interlocks:** Prevent actions when safety conditions aren't met.
- **User validation:** Check current user permissions before allowing actions.

Conditional logic lets your script make decisions based on **what's happening in your system**—like which user is logged in, whether a machine is running, or if a value is too high. In Ignition, conditions are everywhere: in buttons, tags, security, alarms, and more.

Script

```
user = system.security.getUsername()
if user != "admin":
    system.gui.warningBox("Access Denied")

print user
```

user = system.security.getUsername()

- This gets the username of the person currently logged into the system.
- For example, if someone named *Jake* logs in, user becomes "Jake".

if user != "admin":

- This checks if the user is **not** the admin.
- The != operator means "not equal to."
- If the user is not "admin", the code inside the if block will run.

system.gui.warningBox("Access Denied")

- This shows a warning popup saying **"Access Denied"** to any user who isn't the admin.

print user

- This prints the username to the Output Console.
- It helps developers or testers confirm who was logged in.

Why This Is a Common Use Case:

- *It controls who can access sensitive screens or features.*
- *You can easily expand it to check for other users or roles.*
- *This is a foundational way to enforce security using scripting in Ignition.*

Let me know if you want this rewritten to check for user roles instead of just username!

Sample Exercises

Exercise 1: Use if Statement to Monitor a Tag

Objective: Check a tag's value and respond when a threshold is exceeded.

Setup: Create tag [default]Boiler/Pressure with value 88.0

Script

```
pressure = system.tag.readBlocking(["
                        [Site A]Sensors/Sensor 1/Pressure
                        "])[0].value
print pressure

if pressure > 90:
    print "High Pressure Warning!"
else:
    print "Pressure Normal"
```

What You Learn: **How to use a basic if statement to control logic based on a tag's value.**

Exercise 2: Add elif and else Conditions

Objective: Handle multiple states of a tag value using if-elif-else.

Script

```
level = 40  # Assume tank level percentage

if level < 20:
    print "Tank critically low!"
elif level < 70:
    print "Tank level normal."
else:
    print "Tank nearing full capacity."
```

What You Learn: **How to create branching logic that responds to multiple conditions.**

Exercise 3: Nest Conditions for Multi-Criteria Checks

Objective: Use nested if statements to check multiple tag-based inputs.

Setup:

- [Site A]Conveyor/Conveyor1/Running = True
- [default]Conveyor/Load = 80

Script

```
running = system.tag.readBlocking(["
    [Site A]Conveyor/Conveyor1/Running
            "])[0].value
load = system.tag.readBlocking(["
    [Site A]Conveyor/Conveyor1/Load
    "])[0].value


print load

if running:
  if load > 2:
    print "Conveyor is overloaded!"
  else:
    print "Conveyor running normally."
else:
  print "Conveyor is stopped."
```

What You Learn: **How to combine logic from multiple tags for decision making.**

Exercise 4: Use Boolean Tags for Operational Decisions

Objective: Activate logic based on a single true/false condition.

Setup:

- [Site A]Conveyor/Running = False

Script

```
IsRunning = system.tag.readBlocking(["
          [Site A]Conveyor/Conveyor1/Running
                        "])[0].value

If not IsRunning:
    print "Pump is OFF – send technician."
```

What You Learn: How to use not to reverse a boolean and act on false conditions.

Exercise 5: Combine Conditions for Safety Logic

Objective: Trigger a message only if multiple critical conditions are met.

Script

```
temp = 105
pressure = 95

If temp > 100 and pressure > 90:
    print "EMERGENCY: Shut down system immediately!"
```

What You Learn: How to combine multiple and conditions for alarms or shutdown logic.

5

Chapter 05: Control Flow – Loops

Loops in Ignition scripting allow repetitive execution of code, making them essential for tasks like iterating through datasets, writing to multiple tags, or performing batch calculations. The for loop is commonly used to iterate over lists, datasets, or ranges, while the while loop continues executing as long as a condition remains true. Proper use of loops enables efficient automation, reduces redundancy, and supports dynamic processing of multiple values or conditions. Understanding loops is key to writing scalable, flexible scripts in Ignition.

5.1 Using for Loops to Work with Lists and Datasets

for loops are perfect for iterating through datasets, tag paths, or table values in Ignition.

Example – loop through multiple tags:

This script demonstrates how to use a **for loop** in Ignition to iterate through a list of tag paths, read each one, and print its value. It's a common and efficient way to process multiple tags dynamically using scripting.

Script

```
tags = [
    "[Site A]Tank/Tank1/Level",
    "[Site A]Tank/Tank2/Level"
    ]
for tag in tags:
    value = system.tag.readBlocking([tag])[0].value
    print "Tag:", tag, "Value:", value
```

tags = [...]

- This defines a **list** of tag paths. Each string represents the path to a tag in the Ignition tag tree—typically reading a numeric level from different tanks.

for tag in tags:

- This is a **for loop** that goes through each tag path in the list, one at a time. The variable tag will take on the value of each path during each iteration.

value = system.tag.readBlocking([tag])[0].value

- This reads the current value of the tag using readBlocking, which returns a list of qualified values. [0].value extracts the actual value from the first (and only) result.

print "Tag:", tag, "Value:", value

- Prints the tag path and its current value to the console. This is useful for verification, diagnostics, or real-time monitoring in the Script Console.

This approach is commonly used to:

- *Poll multiple tag values at once*
- *Generate summary reports*
- *Validate equipment readings*
- *Dynamically respond to a group of devices or sensors*

By using a loop and a list, the script stays clean, scalable, and adaptable to any number of tags.

5.2 Using while Loops for Repeated Conditions

while loops in Ignition scripting execute a block of code **repeatedly** as long as a specified condition remains true. They are useful when the number of iterations isn't fixed ahead of time. However, in automation scripts (especially in event-driven contexts), they should be used carefully to avoid

infinite loops that can freeze the client or overload the gateway.

Script

```
count = 0
while count < 3:
    print "Running loop", count
    count += 1
```

count = 0

- Initializes a counter variable to 0.

while count < 3:

- The loop will keep running as long as count is less than 3.

print "Running loop", count

- Displays the current value of count during each loop iteration.

count += 1

- Increases count by 1 to eventually stop the loop.

Execution Flow:

1. count = 0 → condition count < 3 is true → prints "Running loop 0"
2. count = 1 → condition count < 3 is true → prints "Running loop 1"

3. count = 2 → condition count < 3 is true → prints "Running loop 2"
4. count = 3 → condition count < 3 is false → loop exits

While loops are powerful but must be used responsibly. If the exit condition is never met (e.g., if count is never incremented), the loop will run forever, potentially freezing the Vision client or causing performance issues in the gateway. Always ensure the loop has a clearly defined exit condition, especially in tag change, timer, or event scripts.

5.3 Using break and continue

The break and continue statements control how loops behave:

- **break**: Immediately exits the loop, even if the loop condition is still true.
- **continue**: Skips the rest of the current iteration and moves to the next one.

Script

```
for I in range(5):
    if I == 3:
        break  # Stop loop at 3
    print "I =", I
```

for i in range(5):

- Creates a loop that iterates through the numbers 0 to 4 (range(5) produces [0, 1, 2, 3, 4]).

if i == 3:

- When the loop variable i equals 3, the condition is met.

break

- The loop is immediately exited, and no further iterations are executed.

print "i =", i

This line runs only if i is **not** 3.

Execution Flow:

- i = 0 → not 3 → prints "i = 0"
- i = 1 → not 3 → prints "i = 1"
- i = 2 → not 3 → prints "i = 2"
- i = 3 → equals 3 → break executes → loop exits

In Ignition scripting, break is useful when:

- *You're scanning a list or dataset and want to exit early after finding a match.*
- *You want to stop processing when a threshold or error condition is met.*

Always use break carefully to maintain control over loop behavior.

5.4 Looping with else Blocks

A lesser-known Python feature: you can add else to a loop. It runs if the loop completes without a break. Here's the full script, including the definition of userList, followed by a clear explanation of how it works:

Script

```
userList = ["operator1", "tech2", "viewer", "guest"]

for user in userList:
  if user == "admin":
    print "Admin found"
    break
else:
  print "No admin in list"
```

userList

· A list of usernames. In this case, it does **not** include "admin".

for user in userList:

· Loops through each username in the list.

if user == "admin":

· Checks whether the current user is "admin".

print "Admin found" and break

· If "admin" is found, prints a message and exits the loop early.

else: (attached to the for loop)

- This else block runs only if the loop completes normally—that is, without hitting break. If "admin" is not found, it prints "No admin in list". Adding "admin" to the list cause the script to output "Admin Found".

This pattern is helpful when searching datasets, user roles, tag lists, or records—especially when you need to detect a specific condition and exit early, or confirm that a value is missing.

5.5 Practical Loop Use Cases in Ignition

- **Bulk tag reads/writes** using tag paths stored in a list
- **Dataset iteration** to check or modify Vision Table data
- **User list filtering** or role-based control
- **Script Console testing** of batch logic

Example – loop over dataset rows:

```
# Define the column names
headers = ["ID", "Name", "Status"]

# Define the row data
rows = [
    [1, "Pump A", "Running"],
    [2, "Pump B", "Stopped"],
    [3, "Pump C", "Running"]
]

# Create the dataset
ds = system.dataset.toDataSet(headers, rows)

# Convert to PyDataSet for easy iteration
pyDS = system.dataset.toPyDataSet(ds)

# Loop through and print each row
for row in pyDS:
    print "ID:", row["ID"], "Name:", row["Name"], "Status:", row["Status"]
```

This script demonstrates how to create and work with a dataset entirely in code—without relying on a component. It's useful for testing, custom scripting, or temporary data handling in Ignition.

A list of column headers for the dataset is defined.

· These names will be the column titles: "ID", "Name", and "Status".

data rows are defined.

· Each inner list represents a row, with values matching the order of the headers.

system.dataset.toDataSet()

- creates a standard Ignition dataset from the headers and rows. This format is used by components like tables, reports, and queries.

Convert the standard dataset to a PyDataSet

- supports Python-style looping and dictionary-like access (e.g., row["Name"]).

Loop through each row and prints its values by referencing columns by name.

This pattern is useful when:

- *Creating sample datasets for testing scripts.*
- *Building data tables dynamically.*
- *Constructing datasets to write to tables, reports, or files.*

It gives you full control over the structure and content of the dataset without needing a UI component.

Sample Exercises

Exercise 1: Loop Through a List of Tag Paths

Objective:

- Read values from multiple tags using a for loop.

Setup:

Create three memory tags:

- [Site A]Motors/Motor 1/Speed
- [Site A]Motors/Motor 2/Speed
- [Site A]Motors/Motor 3/Speed

Script

```
paths = [
        "[Site A]Motors/Motor 1/Speed",
        "[Site A]Motors/Motor 2/Speed",
        "[Site A]Motors/Motor 3/Speed"
        ]
values = system.tag.readBlocking(paths)

for i in range(len(paths)):
   print paths[i], "=", values[i].value
```

What You Learn: How to iterate over tag paths and extract values with index-based loops.

Exercise 2: Loop Through a Dataset Using system.dataset.toPyDataSet()

Objective:

- Iterate through rows in a table dataset using a for loop.

Setup

- **Drag a Table onto a Vision Window.**
- Name it "PumpTable".
- **Manually add some test data** in the Table's data property using the Designer's dataset editor.

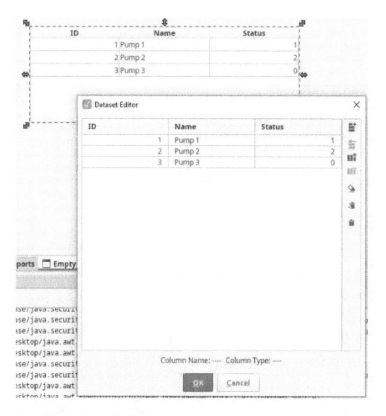

Add a Button to the Window.

- Set the button's actionPerformed event script:

Script:

```
# Get dataset from the table component
rawDS = event.source.parent.getComponent("PumpTable").data

# Convert to PyDataSet
pyDS = system.dataset.toPyDataSet(rawDS)

# Loop through the dataset and print rows
for row in pyDS:
    print "ID:", row["ID"], "Name:", row["Name"], "Status:", row["Status"]
```

What You Learn: How to iterate over PyDatasets and access row values by column name.

Exercise 3: Use a while Loop with a Condition

Objective

· Increment a counter until a threshold is reached.

Script

```
counter = 0
while counter < 5:
    print "Cycle:", counter
    counter += 1
```

What You Learn: How to use while loops for repeated actions based on a condition.

Exercise 4: Loop With Conditional Checks (Alerting)

Objective

- Identify and flag devices with status = "Fault" in a dataset.

Table

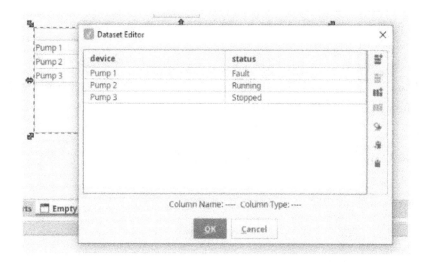

Script

```
table = event.source.parent.getComponent("StatusTable")
data = system.dataset.toPyDataSet(table.data)

for row in data:
  if row["status"] == "Fault":
    print "⚠ Fault detected in", row["device"]
```

What You Learn: How to combine loop iteration with conditional logic.

Exercise 5: Accumulate Values in a Loop

Objective

· Sum column values from a table or dataset.

Table

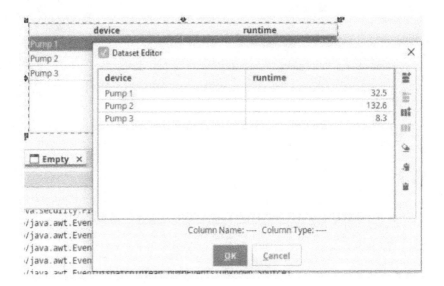

Script

```
table = event.source.parent.getComponent("SummaryTable")
data = system.dataset.toPyDataSet(table.data)

totalRuntime = 0
for row in data:
    totalRuntime += row["runtime"]

print "Total Runtime:", totalRuntime
```

What You Learn: How to perform accumulation logic inside a for loop—useful for totals, averages, etc.

6

Chapter 06: Functions

Functions in Ignition scripting allow you to group reusable blocks of logic under a single name, making code cleaner, more organized, and easier to maintain. Defined using the def keyword, functions can accept parameters, return values, and be called from anywhere in a script. They are especially useful for handling repeated tasks like calculations, tag operations, or decision logic. By structuring automation scripts into functions, you improve readability, reduce duplication, and support modular design across projects.

6.1 Defining Functions to Organize Automation Logic

The function def convertCtoF(celsius): demonstrates how to define a clearly named unit of logic that performs a specific task—in this case, converting Celsius to Fahrenheit. The def keyword introduces the function, followed by the function name and a parameter in parentheses.

Script

```
def convertCtoF(celsius):
    return (celsius * 9.0 / 5) + 32
```

def convertCtoF(celsius):

- This defines a function named convertCtoF that accepts one parameter called celsius.
- The def keyword is used to start a function definition.

return (celsius * 9.0 / 5) + 32

- This line calculates the equivalent Fahrenheit temperature using the standard conversion formula:

F = C × 9/5 + 32

The result is returned to wherever the function is called. For Example:

```
tempF = convertCtoF(25)
print tempF  # Output: 77.0
```

The function is called with the argument 25, and it returns 77.0.

You can define functions in:

- **Project Library scripts** (shared across the project)
- **Script Console** (for testing)
- **Event scripts** (local use)

This pattern is useful when:

- *Converting sensor values (e.g., temperature, pressure, flow).*
- *Encapsulating repetitive calculations.*
- *Keeping logic modular for tag events, transforms, or reporting.*

Functions like this improve clarity and allow scripts to scale cleanly across complex automation projects.

6.2 Passing Arguments and Using Parameters

This script defines a function that accepts **input values (arguments)** and uses them to generate and log a message. It shows how to create a flexible and reusable function by using **parameters** that are replaced with actual values when the function is called. You can pass any data type: numbers, strings, lists, datasets—even tag values or event objects.

Script

```
def logStatus(deviceName, status):
    message = deviceName + " is " + status
    system.util.getLogger("DeviceLogger").info(message)

logStatus("Pump1", "Running")
```

def logStatus(deviceName, status):

- Defines a function named logStatus with two parameters: deviceName and status. These act as placeholders for values that will be passed in when the function is used.

message = deviceName + " is " + status

- Constructs a string by combining the device name and its status. For example, "Pump1 is Running".

system.util.getLogger("DeviceLogger").info(message)

- Sends the constructed message to the Designer's Output Console or logs it under the name "DeviceLogger" in the diagnostics log.

logStatus("Pump1", "Running")

- Calls the function, replacing deviceName with "Pump1" and status with "Running".

Output

```
16:55:34.841 [SwingWorker-pool-1-thread-5] INFO DeviceLogger -- Pump1 is Running
```

This example shows how arguments (like "Pump1") are passed into a function and processed using parameters (deviceName, status). It helps organize messaging or alert logic so you can call it with different values without rewriting the code.

6.3 Returning Values from Functions

This example shows how to define a function that performs a calculation and **returns** the result to wherever the function is called. The return statement is critical when you want the function to produce a value you can store, use, or display elsewhere in your script.

Script

```
def calculateEfficiency(output, Input):
   if Input == 0:
     return 0
   return float(output) / Input * 100

eff = calculateEfficiency(85, 100)
print "Efficiency:", eff
```

def calculateEfficiency(output, input):

- Defines a function that takes two parameters: output and input. These could represent production numbers, energy usage, or any performance metric.

if input == 0:

- Checks for division by zero to avoid an error.

return 0

- If input is zero, the function returns 0 immediately, indicating zero efficiency.

return float(output) / input * 100

- If input is not zero, calculates efficiency as a percentage and **returns** the result to the caller.

eff = calculateEfficiency(85, 100)

- Calls the function with output = 85 and input = 100. The return value (85.0) is stored in the variable eff.

print "Efficiency:", eff

- Prints the result: Efficiency: 85.0

Using return allows you to separate computation logic from display or control logic. It's essential when you need the result of a function for:

- *Further calculations*

- *Conditional decisions*
- *Logging or display*
- *Database writes*

This pattern keeps your automation scripts organized, testable, and scalable.

6.4 Variable Scope: Global vs Local in Ignition Scripts

Variables created inside a function are **local**—they only exist while the function runs. To work with external values, pass them in as parameters or return results. Avoid global variables in automation projects to keep logic safe, predictable, and reusable.

Create a project library script called Scripts and define a function demonstrating local scope and proper variable handling.

Step 1: Open Ignition Designer and Access the Project Library

- Open your project in Ignition Designer.
- In the Project Browser, scroll to the bottom.
- Expand the Scripting section and locate Project Library.
- Right-click Project Library and select New Script.
- Name the script **Scripts** (this is your project script module).

Step 2: Define a Function Inside Scripts

Inside the new Scripts module, add the following function:

- value is a **local variable**, only accessible inside the function.
- The result is **returned**, allowing use elsewhere in your project.

Step 3: Use the Function in a Button or Console

Example (Script Console or a Button's actionPerformed event):

```
x = 5
val = Scripts.multiply(x)
system.gui.messageBox("Result: " + str(val))
```

- x = 5: A local variable defined in the event.
- val = project.Scripts.multiply(x): Calls your reusable function and stores the result.
- system.gui.messageBox(...): Displays the result in a popup window.
- str(val): Ensures the value is converted to a string for display.
- This shows Result: 10 in a message box when the button is clicked.

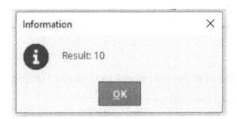

Local scope prevents accidental overwrites and unexpected side effects.

- *Avoid using global variables for state—Ignition scripts run in isolated contexts.*
- *Use project library scripts like Scripts to define clean, reusable functions that take inputs and return outputs.*
- *This approach improves modularity, debuggability, and consistency across your automation project.*

6.5 Using Lambda Functions for One-Line Tasks

A **lambda function** in Python is an anonymous (unnamed) function used for short, simple operations—typically defined in a single line. It's useful when you need a quick function without the overhead of using def.

```
square = lambda x: x * x
print square(4)  # 16
```

lambda x: x * x

- This defines an anonymous function that takes one input (x) and returns x * x. It behaves just like a regular function, but it's written inline.

square = ...

- This assigns the lambda function to a variable named square, so you can call it later like a normal function.

print square(4)

- Calls the square function with 4 as the argument. It returns 16 and prints the result.

Lambda functions are helpful when:

- ***You need a simple transformation inside a script transform in Perspective.***
- ***You're working with list filtering, sorting, or mapping.***
- ***You want to define throwaway functions quickly without adding them to your project script library.***

Important Note:

While useful, lambda functions should be limited to simple tasks. For anything involving multiple steps, logic branches, or error handling, stick with regular def functions for clarity and maintainability.

Sample Exercises

Exercise 1: Define and Call a Simple Function

Objective

· Create a function that prints a device start message.

Script

```
def startDevice(name):
    print name + " has been started."

startDevice("Pump A")
startDevice("Compressor B")
```

What You Learn: How to define and invoke functions with parameters in Jython.

Exercise 2: Return a Computed Result from a Function

Objective

Build a function that calculates average motor speed.

Script

```
def averageSpeed(s1, s2, s3):
    return (s1 + s2 + s3) / 3.0

avg = averageSpeed(1200, 1350, 1100)
print "Average speed:", avg
```

What You Learn: How to use return to pass results from functions.

Exercise 3: Use a Function to Wrap Tag Read Logic

Objective

Create a reusable function to get the current value of a tag.

Script

```
def getTagValue(tagPath):
    return system.tag.readBlocking([tagPath])[0].value

val = getTagValue("[default]Boiler/Pressure")
print "Boiler pressure:", val
```

What You Learn: How to write functions that interact with Ignition tags.

Exercise 4: Pass Data Into a Function and Log Based on Conditions

Objective

- Create a function that checks a temperature and logs status.

Script

```
def checkTemp(temp):
  if temp > 100:
    print "Overheat condition!"
  else:
    print "Temperature normal."

checkTemp(105)
checkTemp(89)
```

What You Learn: How to embed conditional logic inside a function.

Exercise 5: Build a Function That Accepts and Loops Through a Dataset

Objective:

- Write a function that counts how many devices are faulted.

Script (same setup used in Chapter 5 Exercise 4):

```
def countFaults(dataset):
    data = system.dataset.toPyDataSet(dataset)
    faults = 0
    for row in data:
        if row["status"] == "Fault":
            faults += 1
    return faults

table = event.source.parent.getComponent("StatusTable")
faultCount = countFaults(table.data)
print "Faulted devices:", faultCount
```

What You Learn: How to pass datasets into a function, loop through them, and return results.

Chapter 07: Lists

Lists in Ignition scripting are ordered collections of items that can store multiple values in a single variable. They are defined using square brackets ([]) and can hold any data type, including numbers, strings, or even other lists. Lists support indexing, looping, and built-in methods like append(), remove(), and len() for flexible data handling. In automation, lists are useful for managing sets of tag paths, processing datasets, or organizing input values. Mastering lists allows for efficient, dynamic scripting in Ignition projects.

7.1 Creating and Using Lists in Ignition

Creating a List

- You define a list using square brackets [ ]:

```
devices = ["Pump1", "Pump2", "Pump3"]
temperatures = [72.5, 68.0, 75.2]
mixedList = ["Line1", True, 85]
```

- Lists can hold **strings**, **numbers**, **booleans**, or a mix of types.
- You can also create an **empty list**:

```
results = []
```

Accessing List Elements

- Use indexing (zero-based):

```
print devices[0]  # "Pump1"
```

Modifying Lists

· You can change or add items:

```
devices[1] = "Pump2A"    # Modify
devices.append("Pump4")   # Add new item
```

Looping Through a List

· Lists are commonly used with for loops:

```
for device in devices:
    print device
```

Use Cases in Ignition

· Loop through **tag paths**:

```
tagPaths = ["[Site A]Motors/Motor 1/Speed", "[Site A]Motors/Motor 2/Speed"]
for path in tagPaths:
    val = system.tag.readBlocking([path])[0].value
    print path, "=", val
```

- Create dynamic **write operations** using system.tag.writeBlocking()
- Handle rows from a dataset by converting to a PyDataSet and building lists of values.
- Organize names, IDs, or results from user selections or calculations.

Lists in Ignition allow you to group, manage, and process multiple values efficiently. They are versatile, easy to use, and essential for scalable automation scripting. Understanding how to create and use lists is foundational for writing clean, powerful Ignition scripts.

7.2 Common List Operations

You can manipulate lists with basic operations. This script demonstrates how to **dynamically build and manage a list of tag paths** using common list operations (append, insert, remove) in Ignition scripting. It also shows how to loop through the final list and print each path.

Script

```
tagPaths = []

tagPaths.append("[Site_A]Motor1/Speed")     # Add to end
tagPaths.insert(1, "[Site_A]Motor2/Speed")  # Insert at position
tagPaths.remove("[Site_A]Motor2/Speed")     # Remove item
tagPaths.insert(1, "[Site_A]Motor2/Speed")  # Insert at position

for tagPath in tagPaths:
  print tagPath
```

- Line 1 creates an empty list called tagPaths.
- Line 2 adds the string "[Site_A]Motor1/Speed" to the end of the list

using append.

- Line 3 inserts "[Site_A]Motor2/Speed" at position 1 using insert, placing it after the first item.
- Line 4 immediately removes that same item with remove, so the list reverts to having only one item.
- Line 5 inserts "[Site_A]Motor2/Speed" again at position 1.
- Line 6 loops through each item in the list and prints the tag path.
- Line 7 prints the two tag paths in order: Motor1/Speed and Motor2/Speed.

Dynamically building and adjusting lists is useful in Ignition for tasks like batch reading, writing tag values, or generating dynamic logic based on system configuration. It also reinforces list operations like adding, removing, and inserting elements at specific positions.

7.3 Indexing, Slicing, and Ranges

Jython lets you retrieve parts of a list using slice notation:

```
subset = tagPaths[1:3] # Items at index 1 and 2
print tagPaths[:2] # First two
print tagPaths[-2:] # Last two
```

This script demonstrates how to access portions of a list using **indexing**, **slicing**, and **ranges**—tools that are essential when working with subsets of tag paths or any list in Ignition scripting.

- **subset = tagPaths[1:3]** creates a new list containing the items at index 1 and 2. It starts at index 1 and stops just before index 3. This is called slicing.
- **print tagPaths[:2]** prints the first two items in the list—index 0 and

1—by starting at the beginning (no start index) and stopping before index 2.

- **print tagPaths[-2:]** prints the last two items in the list. The -2 index counts from the end, so this slice grabs the two final elements in order.

These operations are useful for extracting parts of a list, analyzing recent or specific entries, or passing subsets into other functions.

You can also generate ranges:

This example demonstrates how to use a range() in a loop to generate a sequence of numbers. The function range(5) produces the values 0 through 4, which are used one by one in the loop.

```
for i in range(5):
print "Row", i
```

This example demonstrates how to use a range() in a loop to generate a sequence of numbers. The function range(5) produces the values 0 through 4, which are used one by one in the loop. For each value, it prints "Row" followed by the current number.

```
Row 0
Row 1
Row 2
Row 3
Row 4
```

In Ignition scripting, range() is often used to loop through dataset rows, indexes in table components, or to apply logic across a set number of iterations. Slices and ranges help you target specific parts of a list or dataset without manually accessing each index.

7.4 Useful List Methods in Ignition Scripting

Lists in Ignition (Jython) include built-in methods and functions that make it easy to **inspect, modify, and evaluate** the contents of the list. These tools are essential when handling tag paths, user inputs, or filtered data sets dynamically.

len(tagPaths) – Count Items

- Returns the number of items in the list.

Script

```
tagPaths = [
    "[Site_A]Motor1/Speed",
    "[Site_A]Motor1/Speed"
    ]

print "Total tags:", len(tagPaths)
```

Output

```
Total tags: 2
```

sorted(tagPaths) – Return a New Sorted List

- Returns a new list with the items sorted alphabetically (does not modify the original).

```
tagPaths = [
    "[Site_A]Motor1/Speed",
    "[Site_A]Motor3/Speed",
    "[Site_A]Motor2/Speed"
    ]

sortedList = sorted(tagPaths)
print sortedList
```

Output

```
['[Site_A]Motor1/Speed', '[Site_A]Motor2/Speed', '[Site_A]Motor3/Speed']
```

tagPaths.reverse() – Reverse the List In-Place

- Modifies the original list by reversing the order of its items.

Script

```
tagPaths = [
    "[Site_A]Motor1/Speed",
    "[Site_A]Motor2/Speed",
    "[Site_A]Motor3/Speed"
    ]

tagPaths.reverse()
print tagPaths
```

Output

```
['[Site_A]Motor3/Speed', '[Site_A]Motor2/Speed', '[Site_A]Motor1/Speed']
```

"[Site_A]Motor1/Speed" in tagPaths – Check Membership

· Returns True if the item exists in the list; otherwise, False.

```
tagPaths = [
    "[Site_A]Motor1/Speed",
    "[Site_A]Motor2/Speed",
    "[Site_A]Motor3/Speed"
    ]

if "[Site_A]Motor2/Speed" in tagPaths:
  print "Motor2 is included"
```

Output

```
Motor2 is included
```

- *Use len() to validate list length before looping or writing values.*
- *Use sorted() to organize tag paths or user entries alphabetically.*
- *Use reverse() when processing values from latest to oldest.*
- *Use in to check if a path, user, or ID exists before processing or writing.*
- *These list methods make scripting in Ignition more flexible, efficient, and reliable.*

7.5 List Comprehensions for Quick Logic

List comprehensions are a compact way to create new lists by processing or filtering items from an existing list—all in a single line. They're useful in Ignition scripting when you need to refine tag paths, extract values, or filter datasets quickly and clearly.

```
tagPaths = [
    "[Site_A]Motor1/Speed",
    "[Site_A]Motor2/Speed",
    "[Site_A]Motor3/Speed"
    ]

filtered = [path for path in tagPaths if "Motor1" in path]
print filtered
```

- This creates a new list called filtered.

- It loops through each item in tagPaths.
- It includes only those items that **contain** "Motor1".
- Equivalent to a for loop with an if condition, but much shorter.

Filter all tag paths related to "Motor1" for a batch read or status display.

Advanced Example

```
tagPaths = [
   "[Site A]Motors/Motor 1/Speed",
   "[Site A]Motors/Motor 2/Speed",
   "[Site A]Motors/Motor 3/Speed"
]

# Read all tag values at once
results = system.tag.readBlocking(tagPaths)

# Build a message with values and quality for each tag
messages = []
for I In range(len(tagPaths)):
   tag = tagPaths[I]
   result = results[I]
   messages.append("Tag: %s\n Value: %s\n Quality: %s" % (tag, result.value,
result.quality))

# Combine messages and show In a message box
finalMessage = "\n\n".join(messages)
print finalMessage
```

- Create a list of three tag paths. Each path is a string that points to a specific tag in the Ignition tag provider [Site A]. These are the tags we want to read.
- Read all three tag values at once using system.tag.readBlocking().
- It takes the list of tag paths as input.

- It returns a list of QualifiedValue objects, one for each tag.
- Each QualifiedValue includes .value, .quality, and .timestamp.
- Initialize an empty list called messages to hold formatted strings.
- Loop through the list of tag paths by index (using range(len(...))).
- tagPaths[i] gives the tag path.
- results[i] gives the corresponding read result.
- result.value is the actual tag value (e.g., motor speed).
- result.quality tells whether the read was successful (e.g., Good).
- The string is formatted and added to the messages list.
- Join all the individual strings in messages into one long string.
- Use two newlines (\n\n) between entries for readability.
- print results

Why This Script Is Useful:

- *It performs an efficient batch tag read in one call instead of three separate ones.*
- *It gives you immediate feedback via text string, useful for testing or diagnostics.*
- *It includes the tag quality, which is essential when troubleshooting.*

Sample Exercises

Exercise 1: Create and Print a List of Device Names

Objective

- Define a list and loop through it to print each item.

Script

```
devices = ["Pump1", "Pump2", "Compressor", "Mixer"]

for device in devices:
    print "Device found:", device
```

What You Learn: How to create a list and iterate over its items.

Exercise 2: Append New Items to a List Dynamically

Objective

· Build a list of active alarms manually.

Script

```
activeAlarms = []

# Simulate condition
alarm1 = True
alarm2 = False

if alarm1:
    activeAlarms.append("High Pressure")

if alarm2:
    activeAlarms.append("Low Flow")

print "Alarms:", activeAlarms
```

What You Learn: How to use .append() to build lists conditionally.

Exercise 3: Read Multiple Tags and Store Values in a List

Setup

- "[Site A]Motors/Motor 1/Speed"
- "[Site A]Motors/Motor 2/Speed"
- "[Site A]Motors/Motor 3/Speed"

```
paths = [
    "[Site A]Motors/Motor 1/Speed",
    "[Site A]Motors/Motor 2/Speed",
    "[Site A]Motors/Motor 3/Speed"
    ]
readings = system.tag.readBlocking(paths)

speeds = []
for result in readings:
  speeds.append(result.value)

print "Speeds:", speeds
```

What You Learn: How to gather tag values into a Python list for later use.

Exercise 4: Filter a List Using a Loop

Objective

- Create a filtered list of devices above a speed threshold.

Script

```
speeds = [1100, 1250, 980, 1450]
fastDevices = []

for speed in speeds:
   if speed > 1200:
      fastDevices.append(speed)

print "Devices exceeding 1200 RPM:", fastDevices
```

What You Learn: How to conditionally filter list items using a loop.

Exercise 5: Use List Indexing and Slicing

Objective

- Access specific elements and subsets of a list.

Script

```
temps = [68, 71, 75, 78, 80, 82]

print "First reading:", temps[0]
print "Last reading:", temps[-1]
print "Middle readings:", temps[2:5]
```

What You Learn: How to use indexing and slicing to extract list elements.

8

Chapter 08: Tuples and Sets

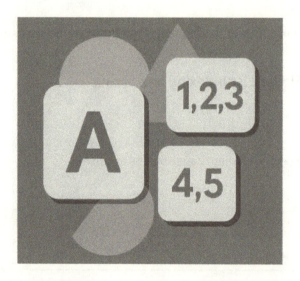

Tuples and sets are two types of collections in Ignition scripting that help organize and manage groups of data. Tuples are immutable sequences, defined with parentheses (()), ideal for fixed groups of values like configuration pairs or constant parameters. Sets are unordered collections of unique elements, defined with curly braces ({}), useful for checking membership and removing duplicates. While tuples maintain order and allow indexing, sets offer fast lookups and are useful in filtering or comparisons. Understanding both helps in writing more precise and efficient scripts in Ignition.

8.1 Tuples: Creating Immutable Sequences

A **tuple** in Python (and Jython) is a sequence of values like a list, but **immutable**, meaning its contents **cannot be changed** after it's created. Once defined, you can access values, but you **can't add, remove, or modify** items in the tuple.

Script

```
statusLevels = ("OK", "Warning", "Fault")
```

- statusLevels is the **name of the tuple** variable.
- The **parentheses ()** define a tuple (unlike a list which uses square brackets []).
- It contains **three string values**: "OK", "Warning", and "Fault".
- These represent a fixed set of **status categories**, often used in alarms or diagnostics

Tuples protect values from accidental changes, which is important for fixed items like:

- *Status levels ("OK", "Fault")*
- *User roles ("Admin", "Operator")*
- *Color definitions (("255", "0", "0") for red)*
- *Coordinate pairs ((x, y))*

Example

```
statusLevels = ("OK", "Warning", "Fault")

currentStatus = "Warning"

if currentStatus in statusLevels:
   system.gui.messageBox("Status is recognized.")
else:
   system.gui.messageBox("Unknown status!")
```

- This checks whether a status is valid based on a fixed list of allowed statuses.
- Tuples ensure that the **reference list stays unchanged** throughout the script.

Tuples are perfect when you need a safe, fixed set of values in your Ignition scripts. Use them when you want to define options or constants that shouldn't be altered, helping keep your logic clean, predictable, and bug-free.

8.2 Tuple Packing and Unpacking

What is tuple packing and unpacking?

- Tuple packing means **grouping multiple values into a single tuple**.
- Tuple unpacking means **extracting those values back into individual variables**.
- This is a powerful feature in Jython that makes your Ignition scripts more elegant, especially when **returning multiple results** from a function.

```
def getExtremes(values):
    return (min(values), max(values))

low, high = getExtremes([2, 7, 1, 9])
print "Min:", low, "Max:", high
```

def getExtremes(values)

- packs two values—**the minimum and maximum**—into a tuple.
- The result of calling getExtremes([2, 7, 1, 9]) is the tuple (1, 9).

low,high = getExtremes([2,7,1,9])

- **unpacks** the two values returned into two separate variables:
- low gets the first value (1)
- high gets the second value (9)

print "Min:",low,"Max:",high

- Displays Min: 1 Max: 9

You can use this pattern in:

- *Gateway scripts to return multiple values (e.g., success flag and message)*
- *Project library scripts to pass multiple results cleanly*
- *Data analysis functions to extract multiple metrics from a datase*

Example

```
# In Scripts
def getFlowRange(data):
   return (min(data), max(data))

# In Vision button or Script Console
flowData = [125, 145, 132, 150]
low, high = Scripts.getFlowRange(flowData)
system.gui.messageBox("Low: %s\nHigh: %s" % (low, high))
```

Tuple packing and unpacking is a concise way to return and handle multiple values in one step. It keeps your code clean, especially in Ignition projects where you often want to pass structured data between scripts.

8.3 Creating and Using Sets

What is a set?

A **set** in Jython is an **unordered collection** that automatically **removes duplicate values**. Unlike lists or tuples, a set guarantees that each item appears **only once**. Sets are especially useful in Ignition for **filtering**, **comparing**, or **deduplicating** values.

```
uniqueUsers = set(["admin", "tech", "admin", "viewer"])
print uniqueUsers  # Output: {'admin', 'tech', 'viewer'}
```

set([...]) converts the list into a set.

- The list contains "admin" twice.
- The resulting set automatically removes the duplicate, storing only one "admin".

print uniqueUsers shows:

- {'admin', 'tech', 'viewer'}
- (Note: sets do **not preserve order**)

Filter unique alarm states:

```
states = ["Fault", "Warning", "Fault"]
uniqueStates = set(states)
```

Remove duplicates from user or role lists:

```
users = ["admin", "viewer", "admin"]
uniqueUsers = set(users)
```

Compare two sets for overlap or difference:

```
allowed = set(["admin", "tech"])
actual = set(["tech", "viewer"])
common = allowed.intersection(actual)  # Result: {'tech'}
```

Sets give you a fast, reliable way to clean up and compare data in Ignition scripting. They're ideal when you need unique values only, such as filtering alarm tags, cleaning up log data, or checking for overlaps between datasets or user permissions. Use set() to simplify logic and avoid manual duplicate checks.

8.4 Performing Set Operations

Set operations allow you to compare groups of values using mathematical logic—intersection, union, and difference. This is especially useful in Ignition scripting when dealing with tag groups, user permissions, alarm states, or any collection of identifiers.

```
setA = set(["Line1", "Line2", "Line3"])
setB = set(["Line2", "Line4"])

print setA & setB  # Intersection: {'Line2'}
print setA | setB  # Union: {'Line1', 'Line2', 'Line3', 'Line4'}
print setA - setB  # Difference: {'Line1', 'Line3'}
```

Intersection (&)

- setA & setB
- Returns items **common to both sets**
- Output: {'Line2'}

Union (|)

- setA | setB
- Combines **all unique items** from both sets
- Output: {'Line1', 'Line2', 'Line3', 'Line4'}

Difference (-)

- setA - setB
- Returns items that are in setA but **not in** setB
- Output: {'Line1', 'Line3'}

Real-World Use Cases in Ignition:

- *Tag comparison: Determine which tags are missing from a second provider*
- *User role filtering: Identify users who are not assigned a required role*
- *Alarm logic: Compare current alarm states against allowed states*

Set operations in Jython offer a fast, readable way to perform group compar-isons. By using & (intersection), | (union), and - (difference), you can efficiently answer questions like: "Which items match?", "What's missing?", and "What's different?"—perfect for scripting in dynamic industrial applications.

8.5 When to Use Tuples vs Sets vs Lists

Understanding the difference between **lists**, **tuples**, and **sets** is crucial when writing clear, efficient Ignition scripts. Each has its own behavior and best use case:

List

- **Use Case:** Ordered collections where you may need to add, remove, or modify items.**Mutable:** Yes – you can change the contents.
- **Ignition Example:** Use lists to manage **tag paths**, **component names**, or **task queues**.

Typical Use:

```
tagPaths = ["[Site A]Motor1", "[Site A]Motor2"]
tagPaths.append("[Site A]Motor3")
```

Tuple

- **Use Case:** Immutable (unchangeable) sequences used for fixed constants or returning multiple values safely.
- **Mutable:** No – contents cannot be modified after creation.
- **Ignition Example:** Use tuples to return **multiple values from a function** or define **fixed categories**.

Typical Use:

```
def getRange(values):
    return (min(values), max(values))
```

Set

- **Use Case:** Unordered collections that automatically remove duplicates — great for **filtering** or **membership checks**.
- **Mutable:** Yes – items can be added or removed.
- **Ignition Example:** Use sets to compare **user roles**, **tag groups**, or **alarm states**.

Typical Use:

```
users = set(["admin", "tech", "admin"])
print users  # {'admin', 'tech'}
```

Type	Use Case	Mutable
List	Ordered data, editable in loops	Yes
Tuple	Fixed constants, safe return values	No
Set	Unique values, filtering comparisons	Yes

In Ignition:

- *Use lists when working with tag paths, datasets, or component IDs that need to be looped or changed.*
- *Use tuples for constants, alarm level pairs, or returning multiple results from a custom function.*
- *Use sets when removing duplicates, checking inclusion, or comparing two groups of items.*

Sample Exercises

Exercise 1: Create and Use a Tuple for Constant Tag Paths

Objective

- Store fixed tag paths in a tuple and read their values.

Setup: Create these tags:

- [Site_A]Boiler/Temp
- [Site_A]Boiler/Pressure

Script

```
tagPaths = ("[Site_A]Boiler/Temp", "[Site_A]Boiler/Pressure")
results = system.tag.readBlocking(tagPaths)

for I In range(len(tagPaths)):
print tagPaths[I], "=", results[I].value
```

What You Learn: How to use immutable tuples to store and access tag paths.

Exercise 2: Use Tuple Unpacking

Objective

- Extract multiple values from a tuple in one line.

Script

```
statusTuple = ("Running", 1420, True)
state, speed, isActive = statusTuple

print "State:", state
print "Speed:", speed
print "Active:", isActive
```

What You Learn: How to unpack tuple values into separate variables.

Exercise 3: Create a Set of Unique Values

Objective

- Eliminate duplicates from a list using a set.

Script

```
devices = ["Pump1", "Pump2", "Pump1", "Pump3", "Pump2"]
uniqueDevices = set(devices)

print "Unique devices:", uniqueDevices
```

What You Learn: How sets automatically remove duplicates from collections.

Exercise 4: Perform Set Operations for Comparison

Objective

- Identify which devices are missing from the expected set.

Script

```
expected = set(["Pump1", "Pump2", "Pump3", "Pump4"])
actual = set(["Pump1", "Pump2", "Pump4"])

missing = expected - actual
print "Missing devices:", missing
```

What You Learn: How to subtract one set from another to find differences.

Exercise 5: Check for Membership Using Sets

Objective

· Test if a value exists in a collection efficiently.

Script

```
faulted = set(["Motor1", "Motor3", "Motor5"])
device = "Motor2"

if device in faulted:
print device + " is faulted!"
else:
print device + " is normal."
```

What You Learn: How to use in with sets for fast membership testing.

9

Chapter 09: Dictionaries

Dictionaries in Ignition scripting are key-value data structures that allow you to store and retrieve data using named keys instead of numerical indexes. Defined using curly braces ({}), each entry consists of a key and a corresponding value (e.g., {"motor": 1}). Dictionaries are ideal for organizing related data, such as tag-value pairs, configuration settings, or device states. Common methods like .get(), .keys(), and .values() support flexible data access and manipulation. Dictionaries are powerful tools for building dynamic, readable, and scalable automation scripts in Ignition.

9.1 Creating and Using Dictionaries

A **dictionary** is a collection of key-value pairs. Each key is **unique**, and it maps directly to a **value**. Dictionaries are ideal in Ignition scripting when you need to quickly look up or organize values by a label, like tag names, device IDs, or user roles.

```
tagValues = {
    "Line1": 85,
    "Line2": 92,
    "Line3": 78
}
```

- tagValues is the name of the dictionary.
- "Line1", "Line2", and "Line3" are **keys** (unique identifiers).
- 85, 92, and 78 are the **values** associated with each key.
- The keys are usually **strings**, but they can be any immutable type (like integers or tuples).

```
print tagValues["Line2"]  # Outputs: 92
```

- You retrieve a value by using its **key** inside square brackets.
- If the key doesn't exist, this will throw an error (unless handled with .get()).

Store tag-value results after a batch read:

```
tags = ["[Site A]Line1/Speed", "[Site A]Line2/Speed"]
values = system.tag.readBlocking(tags)
tagValues = {
   "Line1": values[0].value,
   "Line2": values[1].value
}
```

Map user roles to access levels:

```
access = {
   "admin": "full",
   "operator": "limited",
   "viewer": "read-only"
}
```

Device status config:

```
deviceStatus = {
   "Pump1": "Running",
   "Pump2": "Stopped"
}
```

Dictionaries are ideal when:

- *You need to store associations between identifiers and values.*
- *You want fast lookups based on a name, tag, or ID.*
- *You're handling dynamic data where each item needs a clear label or category.*

In Ignition scripting, dictionaries are powerful tools for creating flexible, readable, and scalable logic—especially when working with tag networks, device maps, or user access controls.

9.2 Accessing and Updating Dictionary Values

Dictionaries in Jython allow you to **modify**, **add**, and **safely retrieve** key-value pairs. This is especially helpful in Ignition when working with dynamic data—like tags, user inputs, or system states—that may change at runtime.

Modifying and Adding Values:

```
tagValues["Line2"] = 95  # Update an existing key
tagValues["Line4"] = 88  # Add a new key-value pair
```

- tagValues["Line2"] = 95 changes the value for the existing key "Line2" from whatever it was (e.g., 92) to 95.
- tagValues["Line4"] = 88 creates a new key "Line4" with the value 88 if it doesn't already exist.

Dictionaries are dynamic, so they grow or change as needed during runtime.

Accessing Values Safely with .get():

```
speed = tagValues.get("Line5", 0)
```

- Tries to get the value for "Line5".
- If "Line5" **exists**, it returns its value.
- If it **doesn't exist**, it returns the **default value** 0 instead of raising a KeyError.

Why This Is Useful in Ignition:

- Avoids script crashes if a tag or config item isn't present.
- Makes it easier to build **dynamic dashboards**, where not all expected data may be available.
- Supports **flexible project scripts** that adapt to new tags or devices without needing changes to the core logic.

Use dict[key] = value to update or add entries.

- *Use dict.get(key, default) to access safely without errors.*
- *This method is ideal when building tag-driven interfaces, alarm displays, or runtime configurations in Ignition.*

9.3 Dictionary Methods for Scripting Efficiency

Dictionaries in Jython offer built-in methods that make automation scripts more efficient and readable. These methods help you **quickly extract**, **loop through**, and **act on** the contents of a dictionary, which is especially valuable in Ignition projects where you're working with tag-value pairs, user-role mappings, or runtime configurations.

```
keys = tagValues.keys()    # Returns a list of all keys
values = tagValues.values() # Returns a list of all values
Items = tagValues.Items()   # Returns a list of (key, value) tuples
```

- .keys() gives you just the **keys** – great if you need to check or compare identifiers.
- .values() gives just the **values** – useful for stats, summaries, or batch processing.
- .items() returns both **keys and values** as pairs – ideal for looping.

Looping with .items():

```
for line, speed in tagValues.Items():
  print "Line:", line, "Speed:", speed
```

- Loops through each key-value pair in the dictionary.
- Assigns the key ("Line1", "Line2", etc.) to line, and its associated value (like 85, 92) to speed.
- Prints both in a formatted message.

Ignition Use Cases:

- **Component binding updates:** Loop through a dictionary of tag names and apply values to matching components.

- **Report generation:** Collect values and labels from dictionaries to dynamically populate reports.
- **Logging and diagnostics:** Output structured status summaries for devices, alarms, or performance metrics.

9.4 Nesting Dictionaries for Structure

Nesting dictionaries means placing one dictionary **inside another**—creating a structured, hierarchical format. This is powerful in Ignition for organizing **multiple attributes per item**, such as status, value, timestamp, or any metadata associated with tags, devices, or users.

```
devices = {
  "Pump1": {"status": "Running", "rpm": 1450},
  "Pump2": {"status": "Stopped", "rpm": 0}
}

print devices["Pump1"]["rpm"]  # Output: 1450
```

devices is the outer dictionary.

- Its keys are device names: "Pump1", "Pump2".
- Each value in devices is **another dictionary** that stores details like "status" and "rpm" for that device.

Accessing devices["Pump1"]["rpm"] means:

- Look up the key "Pump1" in the outer dictionary → returns its inner dictionary.
- Then look up the key "rpm" inside that → returns 1450.

Use Cases in Ignition:

- **Gateway Scripts**: Track device states, last update times, and alarm status.
- **Project Scripts**: Return structured status objects from a function.
- **Data aggregation**: Store multiple tag attributes under a single identifier for display, logging, or analysis.

Looping Through Nested Dictionaries:

```
devices = {
   "Pump1": {"status": "Running", "rpm": 1450},
   "Pump2": {"status": "Stopped", "rpm": 0}
}
for device, info in devices.items():
   print "Device:", device
   print "  Status:", info["status"]
   print "  RPM:", info["rpm"]
```

Output

```
Device: Pump2
  Status: Stopped
  RPM: 0
Device: Pump1
  Status: Running
  RPM: 1450
```

Nesting dictionaries gives your scripts a structured format that mimics real-world hierarchies—like devices with multiple attributes. It's ideal for passing complex results between scripts, storing multi-dimensional tag data, or *managing configurable logic at the Gateway or project level. **This technique** **promotes clarity and scalability in Ignition scripting.***

9.5 Practical Use Cases in Ignition

Dictionaries are powerful tools in Ignition scripting for organizing and managing dynamic logic. Below are common real-world uses and how they streamline automation workflows:

Tag Result Mapping

Use a dictionary to **store tag values** by name after a batch read:

```
tagPaths = ["[Site A]Motors/Motor 1/Speed", "[Site A]Motors/Motor 2/Speed"]
results = system.tag.readBlocking(tagPaths)

tagValues = {}
for I In range(len(tagPaths)):
    tagValues[tagPaths[I]] = results[I].value
    print tagValues[tagPaths[I]]
```

This gives you a dictionary like:

```
{
  "[Site A]Motors/Motor 1/Speed": 1200,
  "[Site A]Motors/Motor 2/Speed": 1180
}
```

User Role Logic

Define access permissions using role-based dictionaries:

```
permissions = {
  "admin": ["view", "edit", "delete"],
  "operator": ["view", "edit"],
  "viewer": ["view"]
}

# Get current user's roles (can be multiple)
userRoles = system.security.getRoles()

# Check if any of the user's roles are allowed to edit
for role in userRoles:
  if "edit" in permissions.get(role, []):
    system.gui.messageBox("Edit access granted.")
    break
else:
  system.gui.messageBox("No edit access.")
```

Component Control in Vision

```
updates = {
  "Tank1": {"value": 80},
  "Tank2": {"value": 95}
}

for name, props in updates.items():
  component = event.source.parent.getComponent(name)
  component.value = props["value"]
```

Script Configuration or Lookup Tables

Store reusable config values:

```
alarmThresholds = {
  "Pump1": 1500,
  "Pump2": 1200
}
```

Or use dictionaries as **code-to-label converters**:

```
statusMap = {
  0: "Stopped",
  1: "Running",
  2: "Fault"
}
```

Writing Tag Values Dynamically

This example performs multiple tag writes using a dictionary:

```
tagMap = {
  "[Site A]Motors/Motor 1/Speed": 100,
  "[Site A]Motors/Motor 2/Speed": 110
}

for path, value in tagMap.items():
  system.tag.writeBlocking([path], [value])
```

- Loops through each tag path and its desired value.
- Writes values using system.tag.writeBlocking().

· Efficient and clean for setting multiple values at once.

Dictionaries offer clarity, flexibility, and performance in Ignition scripting. Use them to:

· *Organize tag interactions*
· *Manage permissions*
· *Dynamically control interfaces*
· *Store config settings*
· *Write or read multiple tags with minimal code*

They're foundational to writing scalable, maintainable automation logic

Sample Exercises

Exercise 1: Create and Print a Simple Dictionary

Objective

· Define a dictionary of device states and print them.

Script

```
devices = {
"Pump1": "Running",
"Pump2": "Stopped",
"Pump3": "Fault"
}

for name in devices:
print name, "is", devices[name]
```

What You Learn: How to create and access key-value pairs in a dictionary.

Exercise 2: Build a Dictionary from Tag Reads

Objective:

· Read multiple tags and store their values in a dictionary.

Setup: Create tags

```
[Site_A]Motors/Motor 1/Speed,
[Site_A]Motors/Motor 2/Speed,
[Site_A]Motors/Motor 3/Speed
```

Script

```
tags = {
"M1 Speed": "[Site_A]Motors/Motor 1/Speed",
"M2 Speed": "[Site_A]Motors/Motor 2/Speed",
"M3 Speed": "[Site_A]Motors/Motor 3/Speed"
}

readings = {}
for label, path in tags.items():
value = system.tag.readBlocking([path])[0].value
readings[label] = value

print readings
```

What You Learn: How to loop through a dictionary and build another with results.

Exercise 3: Update and Add Dictionary Entries

Objective

- Change existing values and add new key-value pairs.

Script

```
status = {"PumpA": "Running", "PumpB": "Stopped"}
status["PumpB"] = "Starting"
status["PumpC"] = "Fault"

print status
```

What You Learn: How to modify and add values in a dictionary dynamically.

Exercise 4: Use a Dictionary to Map Status to Color

Objective

- Use a dictionary as a lookup table for UI logic.

Script

```
statusColor = {
"Running": "green",
"Stopped": "gray",
"Fault": "red"
}

currentStatus = "Fault"
print "Display color:", statusColor[currentStatus]
```

What You Learn: How to use dictionaries for decision-making and visualization.

Exercise 5: Loop Through Keys and Values

Objective

· Print out both keys and values from a dictionary.

Script

```
alarms = {
"Sensor1": "High Temp",
"Sensor2": "Low Pressure",
"Sensor3": "Disconnected"
}

for sensor, msg in alarms.items():
print sensor + " alert:", msg
```

What You Learn: How to iterate over both dictionary keys and values cleanly.

10

Chapter 10: Working with Strings

Strings in Ignition scripting represent sequences of characters used for messages, tag paths, logs, and display values. Defined with quotes (" " or ' '), strings support operations like concatenation (+), formatting, and built-in methods such as .lower(), .replace(), and .split(). They are essential for building dynamic tag references, generating alerts, and formatting data for output. Mastering string manipulation allows you to create flexible and readable scripts that adapt to system variables and user input across Ignition projects.

10.1 String Creation and Concatenation

Strings are one of the most frequently used data types in Ignition scripting. They're essential for creating **messages**, building **tag paths**, updating **labels**, and logging dynamic values. Understanding how to create and manipulate strings is foundational for building responsive, data-driven applications.

Example 1: Concatenating Strings

```
operator = "Charles"
msg = "Current user: " + operator
print msg
```

- Defines a variable operator with the value "Charles".
- Creates a message string by **concatenating** "Current user: " with the operator name using +.

Prints

- Current user: Charles

Example 2: Concatenating Strings with a Number (Using str())

```
temp = 73
log = "Temperature: " + str(temp)
print log
```

- Stores a numeric value 73 in the variable temp.
- Converts the number to a string using str(temp) so it can be safely joined with another string.

Prints:

- "Temperature: 73"

Common Ignition Use Cases:

- **Dynamic tag paths:**

```
motorNum = 1
tagPath = "[Site_A]Motors/Motor " + str(motorNum) + "/Speed"
print tagPath
```

- **Logging values:**

```
# Simulated flow value (replace with tag read in real use)
flow = 158.7

# Create a logger object named "MyScript"
logger = system.util.getLogger("MyScript")

# Log the flow rate as an info-level message
logger.info("Flow rate: " + str(flow))
```

flow = 158.7

· A simulated flow rate value. In practice, you could read this from a tag.

system.util.getLogger("MyScript")

· Initializes a logger named "MyScript" which will appear in the **Diagnostics → Console** log.

logger.info(...)

· Logs the message at the INFO level. The message will look like:

```
09:17:14.164 [SwingWorker-pool-1-thread-7] INFO MyScript -- Flow rate: 158.7
```

Updating component text:

```
# Step 1: Read the speed value from a tag (or simulate)
speed = system.tag.readBlocking(["[Site_A]Motors/Motor 1/Speed"])[0].value
# speed = 123.4  # You can use this line instead if you're simulating

# Step 2: Get the Label component
label = event.source.parent.getComponent("SpeedLabel")

# Step 3: Update its text property
label.text = "Speed: " + str(speed) + " rpm"
```

· *Use + to concatenate strings.*

- *Use str() to convert numbers or other data types into strings before combining.*
- *These techniques make it easy to build dynamic scripts for messages, tag references, alarms, and visual feedback in Vision or Perspective.*

10.3 String Formatting Techniques

When scripting in **Ignition's Jython 2.7 environment**, formatting strings cleanly is essential for building dynamic tag paths, display content, or log messages. However, it's important to know that **not all Python string formatting methods are supported** in Jython.

Recommended: %-Style Formatting (Fully Supported in Jython)

This classic formatting style is fully compatible and reliable:

```
device = "Mixer"
speed = 1200
print "%s is running at %d RPM" % (device, speed)
```

- %s is a placeholder for a string ("Mixer").
- %d is for an integer (1200).

Output

```
>>>
Mixer is running at 1200 RPM
>>>
```

!!!Not Supported: f-Strings

```
# This will fail in Jython
print(f"{device} is running at {speed} RPM")  # SyntaxError in Jython

>>>

SyntaxError: no viable alternative at input '"{device} is running at {speed} RPM"'
(<input>, line 2)
>>>
```

- f-strings are part of Python 3.6+ and are **not available** in Jython 2.7, which is used in Ignition.

Partially Supported: .format()

```
device = "Motor 1"
speed = 101.5
# Works for basic usage
print "{} is running at {} RPM".format(device, speed)  # May work

# Advanced formatting features like alignment or padding may break or behave
unpredictably
```

- While .format() works for simple cases, it's **unreliable** for anything beyond basic use, so it's best avoided in production Ignition scripts.

Safe Alternative: Concatenation with str()

```
pressure = 92.5
message = "Pressure is " + str(pressure) + " psi"
print message
```

- This is simple, clear, and works in all Jython contexts—ideal for building tag paths, messages, or labels.

String Formatting Techniques in Ignition (Jython 2.7)

Method	Supported in Jython?	Recommended?	Description / Notes
% formatting	✅ Yes	✅ Yes	Fully supported. Use `%s` , `%d` , `%.2f` , etc. for clean formatting.
.format()	⚠ Limited	⚠ Use with caution	Works for basic use, but advanced features like alignment may fail.
f-strings	❌ No	❌ Not recommended	Not supported. Will raise a `SyntaxError` in Jython 2.7.
Concatenation + str()	✅ Yes	✅ Yes	Works in all cases. Use for simple messages and when mixing types.

*This quick-reference table helps ensure you're using string formatting methods that are safe and compatible in **Ignition's Jython scripting environment**.*

10.4 Escape Characters and Multiline Strings

In Ignition scripting with Jython, working with **special characters** and **multiline messages** is common when creating alerts, logs, or formatted text for reports. This section covers how to use **escape characters** and **triple-quoted strings** to handle these needs properly.

Escape characters let you include special symbols (like backslashes or quotes) in strings.

```
path = "C:\\Users\\Operator\\Documents"
quote = "He said, \"System Ready.\""

print path
print quote
```

- \\ lets you include a single backslash (\) in file paths or tag names.
- \" allows you to include **quotation marks** inside a string.

Output

```
C:\Users\Operator\Documents
He said, "System Ready."
```

Multiline Strings

- Use **triple quotes** (""" """ or ''' ''') to define strings that span **multiple lines**.

```
message = """Alert:
Pump Overload
Please Reset"""
print message
```

- No need for \n (newline characters)—the line breaks are preserved automatically.
- Useful for writing structured alerts, logs, or formatted display messages.

Output

```
>>>
Alert:
Pump Overload
Please Reset
>>>
```

This format keeps line breaks and spacing exactly as written, making it ideal for:

- **System messages**
- **Alarm details**
- **Log entries**
- **Embedded report text**

Summary Table

Feature	Syntax	Use Case
Escape Backslash	\\	File paths, OPC paths
Escape Quote	\" or \'	Quoting inside strings
Multiline String	""" ... """ or ''' ... '''	Alerts, logs, formatted messages

10.5 Parsing and Splitting Strings

In Ignition scripting, you'll often need to **break down strings** to extract meaningful parts—like **tag names, paths**, or **sensor identifiers**. The .split() method lets you do exactly that, making string parsing easy and efficient.

Example: Splitting a Tag Path

```
tag = "[Site_A]Motors/Motor 1/Speed"
parts = tag.split("/")
print parts[-1]  # Output: Speed
print parts[-2]  # Output: Motor 1
print parts[-3]  # Output: [Site_A]Motors
```

tag.split("/") splits the string wherever it finds a forward slash (/), returning a list:

- ['[Site_A]Motors', 'Motor 1', 'Speed']
- parts[-1] accesses the **last item** in the list—"Speed"—which is the tag's name.

- parts[-2] accesses the **middle item** in the list—"Motor 1"—which is the device name.
- parts[-1] accesses the **first item** in the list—"[Site_A]Motors"—which is the tag's folder path.

Common Use Cases in Ignition:

- Extract tag name from path Get "Speed" from "[Site_A]Motors/Motor 1/Speed"
- Get folder/group from tag path parts[0] gives "[Site_A]Motors"
- Parse CSV values from input "12,45,78".split(",") → ['12', '45', '78']
- Decode barcode or sensor data
- Break structured strings like "P1-123-RUN"

Summary

- *.split(delimiter) breaks a string into a list using the given character.*
- *Use [-1] to grab the last part, [0] for the first, or slice as needed.*
- *It's perfect for dynamically handling tag paths, user inputs, or data strings in automation workflows.*

Sample Exercises

Exercise 1: Concatenate Strings to Build a Tag Path

Objective

- Build a tag path from variable parts and read its value.

Script

```
device = "Motor 1"
property = "Speed"
path = "[Site A]Motors/%s/%s" % (device, property)

result = system.tag.readBlocking([path])[0]
print "Path:", path
print "Value:", result.value
print "Quality:", result.quality
```

What You Learn: How to use string concatenation to dynamically build tag paths.

Exercise 2: Format Strings with Variables

Objective

· Use .format() to build cleaner output messages.

Script

```
temp = 87.4
pressure = 125

message = "Boiler temp: {:.1f} °F, Pressure: {} psi".format(temp, pressure)
print message
```

What You Learn: How to use string formatting to control output style.

Exercise 3: Use String Methods to Process Input

Objective

- Normalize user input using .lower() and .strip().

Script

```
rawInput = " START "
cleanInput = rawInput.strip().lower()

if cleanInput == "start":
    print "Command accepted."
else:
    print "Invalid command."
```

What You Learn: How to clean and standardize input from users or devices.

Exercise 4: Extract Parts of a String

Objective

- Parse a device identifier from a full tag path.

Script

```
path = "[default]Machines/Mixer1/Speed"
parts = path.split("/")

device = parts[-2]
print "Target device:", device
```

What You Learn: How to use .split() and indexing to extract string parts.

Exercise 5: Check for Keywords in Status Strings

Objective

- Detect fault conditions using .find() and in.

Script

```
status = "Overheat Fault Detected"

if "fault" in status.lower():
    print "⚠ Fault detected in system!"
```

What You Learn: How to perform case-insensitive keyword checks in status messages.

11

Chapter 11: Modules and Imports

Modules and imports in Ignition scripting allow you to organize code and reuse functionality by accessing built-in or custom Python libraries. Using the import statement, you can bring in standard modules like math, or custom project scripts stored in shared or project script libraries. This promotes modular design, reduces code duplication, and enables access to specialized tools like date formatting, calculations, or utility functions. Understanding how to use modules effectively improves maintainability and structure in large Ignition scripting projects.

11.1 Using Built-in Modules in Ignition

Ignition scripting, powered by **Jython 2.7**, supports many standard Python modules as well as Ignition-specific modules under the system.* namespace. This allows you to write flexible, powerful scripts for logic, control, logging, data manipulation, and more.

Example 1: Using Python's Built-in math Module

```
import math
print math.sqrt(16)  # Outputs: 4.0
```

- Imports the standard math module.
- Calls math.sqrt(16) to compute the square root of 16.
- This works inside any scripting scope (Vision, Gateway, Perspective).

Example 2: Using Ignition's system.util.getLogger

```
system.util.getLogger("MyScript").info("Script started")
```

- Uses Ignition's built-in scripting library to create a logger named "MyScript".
- Sends an INFO-level message to the Diagnostics console.
- Great for debugging and monitoring script execution.

Other Useful Built-in Modules (Jython 2.7-Compatible)

Module	Use Case	Example
datetime	Date/time manipulation	datetime.datetime.now()
random	Generate random numbers	random.randint(1, 10)
re	Regular expressions (pattern matching)	re.search(r"\d+", "Pump123")
string	String utilities and constants	string.ascii_uppercase
time	Delays, timestamps, or performance timing	time.sleep(1)

- Some CPython modules (like os, subprocess, or threading) may be **limited or unavailable** in Jython due to JVM sandboxing.
- Always test modules in the **Script Console** to ensure compatibility.

Summary:

- *You can combine Python's built-in modules with Ignition's system.* modules to build robust scripts.*
- *Use math, datetime, random, and re for standard logic.*
- *Use system.util, system.tag, system.gui, etc. for Ignition-specific tasks.*
- *Always validate module support when scripting in Jython 2.7.*

11.2 Creating Custom Project Scripts (Script Modules)

Ignition allows you to create **custom project-level script modules** so you can define reusable functions and keep your code organized. These are stored under the **Project Browser → Scripting → Script Library** and can be accessed throughout the project—from event handlers, tag scripts, Perspective views, and more.

Step-by-Step: Creating a Custom Script Module

1. Navigate to Script Library

In the Ignition Designer:

- Go to **Project Browser → Scripting → Script Library**
- Right-click on "Script Library" and choose **New Script**
- Name it utilities

2. Create a Function

Inside the new utilities script, enter:

```
def formatTemp(tempC):
    return (tempC * 9.0 / 5) + 32
```

Using the Script in Other Code

Now that formatTemp is defined in utilities, you can use it anywhere in your project like this:

```
from utilities import formatTemp
print formatTemp(22)  # Outputs: 71.6
```

Summary:

- *Script modules are organized like Python packages.*
- *Each script file becomes an importable module.*
- *This allows you to build a clean, hierarchical structure like:*

- *utilities.formatTemp*
- *utilities.conversions*
- *utilities.alerts*

1.3 Import Styles and Conventions

You can import entire modules, individual functions, or assign aliases for convenience—but some styles are preferred over others, especially in automation environments.

Importing the Whole Module

```
Import math
print math.sqrt(16)
```

- Most readable.
- Makes it clear where each function comes from (math.sqrt).

Importing a Specific Function

```
from math Import sqrt
print sqrt(16)
```

- Good when you only need a few functions.
- Use with care: avoids full module prefix, but risks name conflicts if not used carefully.

Using an Alias

```
import system.util as util
util.getLogger("MyScript").info("Running")
```

- Cleaner when using long module names like system.util.
- Makes code shorter and still understandable.
- Common in larger scripts with many Ignition system modules.

Avoid Wildcard Imports!

```
from math import *
```

DON'T DO THIS!!

- Not recommended in Ignition scripting.
- Pollutes the namespace — you can't tell where a function came from.
- Can override existing functions unintentionally.
- Harder to debug and maintain.

*In Ignition scripting using Jython, the best practice for importing modules is to favor clarity, consistency, and maintainability over brevity. Always use explicit imports rather than wildcard imports. This means you should generally use import module or from module import function for only what you need, and avoid from module import *, which clutters the namespace and can lead to unpredictable conflicts.*

For example, importing the entire module like import math and then calling math.sqrt(16) is clear and traceable. If you're using only one or two functions repeatedly, importing them directly (e.g., from math import sqrt) is acceptable, but you should be cautious not to overwrite or shadow other names in your script. Using aliases like import system.util as util is a good practice when working with long module names, as it keeps your code readable and concise.

Ultimately, avoid wildcard imports entirely, especially in Ignition, as they reduce code clarity and increase the risk of name collisions. Stick to well-scoped, purposeful imports to ensure your automation scripts remain clean, easy to debug, and scalable.

11.4 Best Practices for Organizing Script Modules

A well-structured script library in Ignition makes your project more maintainable, testable, and team-friendly. Rather than placing all logic in event handlers or tag scripts, you should create a clean set of **modular, reusable project scripts** grouped by purpose.

Here are the best practices:

Group by Function

Organize your script modules by **purpose or category**, rather than mixing unrelated logic.

Examples:

- logging.py – handles custom logging utilities
- calculations.py – contains math or unit conversion functions
- userOps.py – manages user validation, permissions, or sessions
- alerts.py – reusable alarm-handling logic

This separation makes it easy to find and update functions without impacting unrelated logic.

Keep Scripts Short and Focused

Each function should have **one clear responsibility**. Avoid large functions that try to do too much. This makes testing and debugging easier and encourages reuse across Vision, Perspective, and Gateway scopes.

Use Naming Conventions

- Use **lowercase module names** like mathutils, alerts, tagtools.
- Use **descriptive, snake_case function names** like calculate_pressure_ drop() or send_user_alert().

This aligns with Python standards and improves readability.

Comment Generously

Document:

- **What the function does**
- **Expected inputs and outputs**
- **Side effects**, like writing tags or launching popups

This is especially important in **Gateway Event Scripts** or shared project utilities where behavior isn't immediately visible.

Example:

```
def formatTemp(celsius):
    """
    Converts Celsius to Fahrenheit.
    Args:
        celsius (float): Temperature in Celsius.
    Returns:
        float: Converted temperature in Fahrenheit.
    """
    return (celsius * 9.0 / 5) + 32
```

Test in the Script Console

Before using any function in production:

- Run it in the Script Console to confirm it returns the expected result
- Log output with system.util.getLogger() if needed
- Use test functions (e.g., def test():) in your module for self-validation

Summary

Good script organization makes your Ignition project:

- *Easier to scale*
- *Easier to debug*
- *More collaborative across teams*

Stick to modular, well-documented, purpose-driven scripting — and your automation logic will be cleaner, safer, and more efficient. Let me know if you'd like a template layout for a large project!

Sample Exercises

Exercise 1: Import a Built-in Ignition Library

Objective:

· Use the system.date module to get and format the current time.

Script:

```
import system.date

now = system.date.now()
formatted = system.date.format(now, "yyyy-MM-dd HH:mm:ss")
print "Current time:", formatted
```

What You Learn: How to import and use built-in Ignition modules.

Exercise 2: Use a Java Class with import

Objective:

· Use a Java class inside a Jython script to manipulate time.

Script:

```
from java.util import Calendar

cal = Calendar.getInstance()
year = cal.get(Calendar.YEAR)
print "Current year:", year
```

What You Learn: How to access Java classes using import in Ignition's Jython engine.

Exercise 3: Create a Custom Script Module and Import It

Objective:

- Define a reusable function in a script module and use it from a component.

Steps:

- Go to Project > Scripting > Script Library.
- Add a new script module called utilities.
- Add this code:

```
def welcome(name):
return "Welcome, " + name + "!"
```

From a button's actionPerformed event, call:

```
import Utilities
msg = Utilities.welcome("Operator A")
system.gui.messageBox(msg)
```

What You Learn: How to create and use your own script modules in a project.

Exercise 4: Organize Project Scripts Using Naming Conventions

Objective:

- Simulate organized script structure by grouping related functionality under logical module names using consistent naming patterns.

Steps:

Open the Ignition Designer.

- Go to **Project Browser → Scripting → Script Library**.
- **Create a new script module.**
- Right-click **Script Library**, click **New Script**, and name it:

```
utilities_logging
```

- Script names must be flat — this simulates utilities/logging.py by using an underscore (_) to group them.

Add this code inside utilities_logging:

```
def log_info(message):
    """
    Logs an info-level message with a standard tag.
    """
    system.util.getLogger("Utilities").info("[INFO] " + message)

def log_error(message):
    """
    Logs an error-level message with a standard tag.
    """
    system.util.getLogger("Utilities").error("[ERROR] " + message)
```

Test It in the Script Console:

```
import utilities_logging
utilities_logging.log_info("This is a test message.")
utilities_logging.log_error("This is an error test.")
```

What You Learn: How to organize larger projects into for clarity and reuse.

12

Chapter 12: File I/O

File I/O in Ignition scripting enables reading from and writing to files for data exchange, logging, or external storage. Using built-in Python functions like open(), read(), write(), and close(), scripts can interact with local or network file systems (typically in Gateway scope). File I/O is useful for exporting reports, importing configuration data, or saving diagnostic logs. Proper handling, including using with blocks and checking paths, ensures safe and efficient file operations within Ignition's scripting environment.

12.1 Reading and Writing Files in Ignition

In Ignition, **file access is tightly controlled** and depends on the **script's scope** — whether it runs in a **Vision Client**, **Designer**, or on the **Gateway**. Unlike standard Python, you should avoid using native open() functions and instead use Ignition's built-in system.file methods for safe and consistent behavior.

Writing a File (Client or Designer Scope)

```
system.file.writeFile("C:/Logs/data.txt", "System check complete.")
```

- Writes the given text into the file at the specified path.
- Will **overwrite the file** if it exists.
- You can pass a 1 as the third parameter to **append** instead of overwrite:

```
system.file.writeFile("C:/Logs/data.txt", "Log entry.\n", 1)
```

Scope Restrictions (Very Important)

- **ScopeCan Access Local Files?Notes**

Designer

- Yes
- Full access to the designer machine's filesystem

Vision Client

- Yes
- Accesses the client machine's filesystem (user-facing)

Gateway

- No (not by default)
- Gateway runs on the server; use system.file.writeFile only with proper configuration or use java.io.* carefully and securely

Best Practices:

- Always use **absolute paths** when testing in Designer or Client.
- For Gateway file access, consider using **shared folders**, **network paths**, or **database logging** instead.
- Never rely on local file access in Gateway event scripts without validating your environment.

Use system.file.readFileAsString() and system.file.writeFile() for safe file I/O.

- *Works only in Vision or Designer — not Gateway scripts.*
- *Scope matters — test in the right context and always verify path access before production use.*

Reading a File (Client or Designer Scope)

```
filePath = "C://Logs//data.txt"
text = system.file.readFileAsString(filePath)
print text
```

Note the extra slash is required for the string to work

- Reads the entire contents of a local file as a string.
- Works only in **Vision Clients** or the **Designer**, not in Gateway scripts.
- Useful for loading configuration, logs, or templates.

12.2 Using File Dialogs for User Interaction

In **Ignition Vision**, when you need the user to select or save a file on their local machine, you can use **Ignition's built-in file dialog functions** from the system.file library. These dialogs only work in **Vision Clients** or the **Designer**, and are perfect for exporting data, selecting templates, or saving reports.

Open File Dialog (Let User Choose a File to Read)

```
filePath = system.file.openFile()
if filePath:
    content = system.file.readFileAsString(filePath)
    print content
```

- system.file.openFile() shows a native file picker to the user.
- Returns None if canceled.
- If a file is selected, it reads and prints the content using readFile-AsString().

Save File Dialog (Let User Choose Where to Save)

```
savePath = system.file.saveFile()
if savePath:
    system.file.writeFile(savePath, "Data exported successfully.")
```

- system.file.saveFile() opens a dialog prompting the user to select a save location.
- Returns None if canceled.
- The selected file path is then used with writeFile() to save content.

Use Case Examples in Vision:

- **Exporting a table** as CSV or Excel
- **Saving a configuration** from a form
- **Allowing user to load a template** or document
- **Viewing logs** or importing data

Use system.file.openFile() and system.file.saveFile() to create intuitive, user-driven file workflows in Vision Clients. They're safe, flexible, and simplify tasks like report saving, data logging, and configuration exports — while respecting the user's file system access and preferences.

12.3 Reading CSV Files for Automation Tasks

In Ignition, you can read CSV files using the **Vision file picker** and simple string manipulation. This makes it easy to load structured data like **tag configurations**, **batch processing values**, or **control parameters** into your system from a user-selected file.

```
path = system.file.openFile("csv")
If path:
  data = system.file.readFileAsString(path)
  rows = data.split("\n")
  for row in rows:
    fields = row.split(",")
    print fields
```

- **system.file.openFile("csv")**: Opens a file dialog filtered to show only .csv files.
- **system.file.readFileAsString(path):** Reads the selected file's contents as a single string.
- **split("\n")**: Breaks the file into rows.
- **split(",")**: Splits each row into comma-separated fields.
- **Use strip() to clean whitespace or trailing characters:** fields = row.strip().split(",")
- **Skip blank or malformed rows:** if len(fields) >= expected_field_count

Reading CSV files in Ignition using system.file.openFile() and readFileAsString() is a powerful way to bring in structured external data. Whether you're configuring tags, running batch jobs, or syncing external systems, this method gives you a flexible, user-driven import workflow in Vision Clients.

12.4 Handling Exceptions During File Access

When performing file operations in Ignition, errors can happen due to missing files, permission issues, or path problems. To keep your application stable and user-friendly, you should always use try/except blocks and log any exceptions for troubleshooting.

Basic Exception Handling Example

```
try:
  content = system.file.readFileAsString("C:/badpath.txt")
except:
  system.gui.messageBox("Failed to open file.")
```

- Wraps the file read call in a try block.
- If the file doesn't exist or access fails, the except block runs.
- system.gui.messageBox() shows a friendly error to the user in Vision or the Designer.

Add Logging for Traceability

- You should also log exceptions so developers can diagnose the issue later:

```
logger = system.util.getLogger("FileOps")

try:
  content = system.file.readFileAsString("C:/badpath.txt")
except Exception as e:
  system.gui.messageBox("Failed to open file.")
  logger.error("File read failed: " + str(e))
```

- getLogger("FileOps") creates a named logger.
- logger.error() records the exact error message to the Designer's Output

Console or logs, helping you track down the problem.

Tips for Robust File Handling:

- Always **assume file access can fail** — especially on client machines with unpredictable file systems.
- Catch Exception as e to access the error message.
- Use logger.info() or logger.debug() to trace file paths and execution steps.
- Avoid silent failures — either notify the user or log clearly.

Summary:

Exception handling during file access is essential for creating reliable Ignition Vision applications. Use try/except to catch failures, notify the user when necessary, and log details for maintainability and debugging.

Let me know if you'd like to write a reusable file utility function that wraps reads and logs errors automatically!

12.5 File I/O Best Practices – Guidelines for Safe Automation

When working with file input/output in Ignition, it's crucial to follow platform-aware best practices to ensure safety, stability, and compatibility across client machines and server environments. Here's how to handle files properly across different contexts:

Scope Matters

- **Only Vision Clients and the Designer** can interact with the local file system using system.file.*.
- **Gateway scripts cannot read or write local files** on the client's machine.
- For server-side access in Gateway scripts, use secure workarounds (e.g.,

mapped drives, database storage, or Web Dev endpoints).

Never Use Python's open() Function

- Avoid using open(), read(), write() — these are **not reliable** in Jython under Ignition and may violate scope rules.

Always use Ignition-safe methods like:

- system.file.readFileAsString()
- system.file.writeFile()
- system.file.openFile()
- system.file.saveFile()

Use File Dialogs Instead of Hardcoded Paths

- Avoid hardcoding file paths like C:/Logs/output.txt in production.

Use:

- system.file.openFile() for user-selected input
- system.file.saveFile() for user-defined output locations
- This improves portability and user control — especially when projects run across multiple client machines.

Validate User Input

- Always verify file extensions, content format, and structure when importing files.
- Example: if expecting a CSV, check .endswith(".csv") and inspect headers or row count before processing.
- Sanitize filenames if reusing them to create new files.

Secure Gateway File Access

If you must access files from a Gateway script, you have two main options:

- Use a shared network path (e.g., \\server\shared\folder) that the Gateway has access to.
- Expose a secure **Web Dev endpoint** to upload or download files via HTTP.

Sample Exercises

Exercise 1: Save a Simple Log File to Disk (Client Scope)

Objective:

- Write a string to a text file on the local system using Vision scripting.

Script (use in a Vision button's actionPerformed event):

```
path = system.file.saveFile("log.txt")
if path:
    text = "System check completed at startup."
    system.file.writeFile(path, text)
    system.gui.messageBox("Log saved to: " + str(path))
```

What You Learn: How to use system.file.saveFile() and system.file.writeFile() to save local files from a Vision Client.

Exercise 2: Read and Display a File's Contents

Objective:

· Load a text file and show its contents to the user.

Script:

```
path = system.file.openFile("txt")
if path:
content = system.file.readFileAsString(path)
system.gui.messageBox("File Contents:\n" + content)
```

What You Learn: How to open and read a file's content using Vision Client scripts.

Exercise 3: Write Multiple Lines to a File

Objective:

· Create a multi-line status report and write it to disk.

Script:

```
lines = [
"Ignition System Report",
"---------------------",
"All devices online.",
"No alarms present.",
"Last checked: " + system.date.format(system.date.now(), "yyyy-MM-dd
HH:mm:ss")
]

path = system.file.saveFile("report.txt")
If path:
system.file.writeFile(path, "\n".join(lines))
```

What You Learn: How to write structured data into a text file.

Exercise 4: Export Dataset to CSV (Vision Table Component)

Objective:

· Export a table's dataset to a CSV file.

Script:

```
table = event.source.parent.getComponent("MyTable")
data = table.data
path = system.file.saveFile("table_export.csv")

if path:
system.file.writeFile(path, system.dataset.toCSV(data))
system.gui.messageBox("Exported table to CSV.")
```

What You Learn: How to convert a dataset to CSV and export it.

13

Chapter 13: Error Handling

Error handling in Ignition scripting ensures your code responds gracefully to unexpected issues, such as missing tags, failed queries, or invalid data. Using try, except, and optionally finally blocks, you can catch exceptions, log errors, and maintain system stability without crashing scripts. This approach is essential for debugging, alerting operators, and creating fault-tolerant automation logic. Effective error handling improves script reliability, simplifies troubleshooting, and ensures robust behavior in real-time Ignition applications.

13.1 Introduction to Exceptions in Ignition

In any Ignition project, scripting involves interacting with dynamic systems — tag values, user inputs, datasets, and files — all of which can fail unexpectedly. When something goes wrong, such as a missing tag or a bad dataset reference, Ignition does not crash the system but instead allows you to **catch and handle errors** using Python's standard try/except structure.

An **exception** is an error that occurs at runtime, interrupting the normal flow of your script. If left unhandled, it can cause your event, function, or binding to stop prematurely. By catching exceptions, you can **log them, notify users, or apply fallback logic** — making your application more resilient.

For example, if you attempt to read a tag that doesn't exist, you might not get an immediate error — but the result could be invalid or unusable. Instead of assuming everything will succeed, wrap your logic with a try/except block to safeguard your script.

This sets the foundation for using try/except, while **Section 13.2** can then dive into the practical application and patterns for using it effectively.

✏ Common Exceptions in Ignition Scripting

Scenario	Potential Issue	Suggested Exception Type	Example Response
Tag read/write	Bad path, tag not found	No exception unless checked	Check `result.quality.isGood()` manually
User input (empty/missing field)	`None` or invalid value	`ValueError`	Raise if required field is empty
Component property access	Component not found	`AttributeError`, `KeyError`	Catch and display error in Vision
Dataset access	Bad index, missing column	`IndexError`, `KeyError`	Wrap access in `try/except` to avoid hard failures
File operations	File not found, no permission	`IOError`, `OSError`	Show error message, log failure
Division or type conversion	Divide by zero, bad cast	`ZeroDivisionError`, `TypeError`	Validate inputs before math or casting
Script module import/use	Bad reference or missing module	`ImportError`, `NameError`	Check project script name and scope

13.2 Using try/except Blocks – Defensive Scripting in Ignition

In Ignition, wrapping your code in try/except blocks helps protect your application from unexpected runtime errors. This is especially important when handling user input, accessing components, or interacting with tags and datasets — where errors are common.

```
try:
    result = system.tag.readBlocking(["[default]Bad/Tag"])[0]
    if not result.quality.isGood():
        raise Exception("Bad tag quality: " + str(result.quality))
    value = result.value
except Exception as e:
    system.gui.warningBox("Tag read failed: " + str(e))
```

try:

- Begins a try block. You're saying: "Try to execute the following lines, but if something goes wrong, catch it."

result = system.tag.readBlocking(["[default]Bad/Tag"])[0]

- Calls readBlocking() to read a tag value synchronously.
- Even if the tag is bad or doesn't exist, this **does not throw an error** — instead, it returns a QualifiedValue object.
- [0] accesses the first (and only) item from the result list.

if not result.quality.isGood():

- Checks whether the quality of the tag read is good.
- If the tag path doesn't exist, the quality will be something like "Bad_NotFound" or "Bad_Unknown".
- .isGood() returns False for these, so this line is your **manual error detection**.

raise Exception("Bad tag quality: " + str(result.quality))

- Manually raises an exception if the tag read quality is bad.
- This forces the flow to jump to the except block.

value = result.value

- If the quality is good, this line runs and stores the actual tag value in the value variable.

except Exception as e:

- This block **catches any exceptions** raised in the try block — including the one you manually raised.
- The exception message (such as "Bad tag quality: Bad_NotFound") is stored in variable e.

system.gui.warningBox("Tag read failed: " + str(e))

- Displays a **popup warning box** in the Vision Client (or Designer Preview) with the error message.
- Helps alert the user to the failure.

This script safely reads a tag and manually checks for bad quality. If the tag doesn't exist or has a bad status, it raises an exception, which triggers the except block to show an error message to the user. This is the proper way to treat tag read failures like actual errors in Ignition scripting.

13.3 Using finally for Cleanup in Ignition

The finally block in Python always executes — **regardless of whether an error occurred** in the try block. In Ignition scripting, this is especially useful for ensuring critical cleanup actions still happen, such as **resetting tag values**, **closing resources**, or **logging results**, even if something in your logic fails.

Example: Tag Reset with finally

```
try:
  system.tag.writeBlocking("[Site A]Pump/Start", [1])
except:
  system.gui.warningBox("Start command failed")
finally:
  system.tag.writeBlocking("[Site A]Pump/Start", [0])
```

- The script attempts to write 1 to start a pump.
- If the write fails, an error message is shown.
- Regardless of success or failure, finally resets the tag back to 0.

Common Use Cases for finally in Ignition

Reset control signals

‣ Avoid leaving equipment in an unintended state

Log success or failure

‣ Guarantee that audit entries or diagnostics are always recorded

Close file or database connections

‣ Prevent resource leaks and keep the system stable

Turn off temporary flags

‣ Ensure UI indicators or tag overrides are cleared after execution

Unlock logic paths

▸ Release holds or manual overrides even if an error occurs

Using a finally block ensures post-operation cleanup runs no matter what, making your scripts safer and more reliable — especially when dealing with equipment, tag control, or automation steps that must complete or reset correctly.

13.4 Raising Your Own Exceptions – Enforcing Rules in Ignition Scripts

In addition to catching exceptions, you can also **raise your own** to enforce rules, guard against invalid conditions, or halt execution when something critical is wrong. This is especially valuable in industrial applications where **violating safety limits, running commands out of sequence, or processing bad data** could cause real-world consequences.

Basic Example

```
Itemp = 120
if temp > 100:
    raise Exception("Temperature exceeds safety threshold")
```

This immediately stops the script and throws an error that can be caught with try/except.

When to Raise Exceptions in Ignition

To prevent unsafe operations

- Raise if machine speed, temperature, or pressure exceeds configured limits.

To validate input

- Catch bad user input or missing form fields before continuing logic.

To block invalid workflow

- Enforce that steps must be followed in order (e.g., cannot start batch without confirming materials).

To stop database writes

- Abort inserts or updates if required values or references are missing.

Example: Validating User Entry

```
username = event.source.parent.getComponent("UsernameField").text
if not username:
    raise ValueError("Username is required")
```

Example: Enforcing Tag Precondition

```
valveStatus = system.tag.readBlocking(["[default]Valve/Open"])[0].value
if not valveStatus:
    raise Exception("Cannot start pump while valve is closed")
```

Best Practices

- Use **descriptive error messages** so your exception tells you *what* went wrong and *why*.
- Raise **specific exception types** (ValueError, TypeError, RuntimeError) when appropriate for better control and filtering.
- Combine raise with try/except to create **clean, guarded logic** — raise the problem, catch it, and respond gracefully.

13.5 Logging Errors with system.util.getLogger()

In Ignition, not all errors are visible to users — especially in **Gateway Timer Scripts**, **Tag Change Scripts**, and **Perspective or Vision background tasks**. To monitor and debug these scripts, you should use system.util.getLogger() to **log messages, errors, and variable states** during execution.

Example: Logging a Tag Read Error

```
logger = system.util.getLogger("PumpControl")

try:
    result = system.tag.readBlocking(["[Site A]Pump/Start"])[0]
    if not result.quality.isGood():
        raise Exception("Bad tag quality: " + str(result.quality))
    value = result.value
except Exception as e:
    logger.error("Pump status read failed: " + str(e))
```

- result = ... returns a QualifiedValue, not an error.

- result.quality.isGood() checks if the tag read was successful.
- If it wasn't, you manually raise Exception() so the except block runs.
- The logger now captures and records the failure.

No exception is thrown:

- *readBlocking() always returns a result, even if the tag path is invalid or unreadable.*

You must check the quality manually:

- *Use result.quality.isGood() to determine whether the tag read was successful.*

Raise an exception yourself if needed:

- *If the quality is bad, use raise Exception() to trigger error handling or logging.*

Sample Exercises

Exercise 1: Basic try/except Around Tag Read

Objective:

- Handle an error that may occur when reading a non-existent tag.

Script:

```
try:
    result = system.tag.readBlocking(["[default]NonexistentTag"])[0]
    if not result.quality.isGood():
        raise Exception("Bad tag quality: " + str(result.quality))
    value = result.value
    print "Tag value:", value
except Exception as e:
    print "Error reading tag:", str(e)
```

What You Learn: How to catch and log errors when tag paths are incorrect or unavailable.

Exercise 2: Handle Division by Zero Gracefully

Objective:

• Prevent runtime failure from a division error.

Script:

```
numerator = 100
denominator = 0

try:
result = numerator / denominator
print "Result:", result
except ZeroDivisionError:
print "Cannot divide by zero!"
```

What You Learn: How to catch specific exceptions like ZeroDivisionError.

Exercise 3: Use finally to Clean Up After File Access

Objective:

- Ensure a message is logged whether the script succeeds or fails.

Script:

```
try:
    path = system.file.openFile("txt")
    if path:
        content = system.file.readFileAsString(path)
        print content
except Exception as e:
    print "Error reading file:", str(e)
finally:
    print "File read operation complete."
```

What You Learn: How to use finally to execute clean-up logic regardless of success or failure.

Exercise 4: Use Error Logging in Gateway Scope

Objective:

- Log detailed errors from Gateway scripts to help with debugging.

Script:

```
logger = system.util.getLogger("TagHealthCheck")

try:
value = system.tag.readBlocking(["[default]Pump/Speed"])[0].value
logger.info("Pump speed read: " + str(value))
except Exception as e:
logger.error("Failed to read pump speed: " + str(e))
```

What You Learn: How to integrate try/except with system.util.getLogger() for production-ready logging.

Exercise 5: Catch Multiple Types of Errors

Objective:

· Respond differently based on the type of error encountered.

Script:

```
ltry:
userInput = int("abc") # Will raise ValueError
except ValueError:
print "Please enter a valid number."
except Exception as e:
print "Unexpected error:", str(e)
```

What You Learn: How to handle specific and generic errors appropriately in scripting logic.

14

Chapter 14: Introduction to Classes and Objects

Classes and objects in Ignition scripting introduce the basics of object-oriented programming, allowing you to create reusable, structured representations of real-world entities. A class defines a blueprint with properties and methods, while an object is an instance of that class. This approach helps organize complex logic, such as modeling equipment, alarms, or batches.

Using classes promotes modularity, code reuse, and clarity, making it easier to manage and scale scripts in Ignition projects.

14.1 Defining Your Own Classes

Jython supports object-oriented programming, allowing you to define **custom classes** to model real-world systems. While many Ignition scripts are procedural, classes are useful for **grouping related logic**, **organizing data**, or **building reusable utility tools** — especially in shared project scripts.

Example: Defining a Pump Class

```
class Pump:
  def __init__(self, name, rpm):
    self.name = name
    self.rpm = rpm
```

- **class Pump:** defines a new class named Pump.
- ___init___ is the constructor method, called when a new object is created.
- self.name and self.rpm are attributes assigned at creation.

Why Use Classes in Ignition?

- Model devices like **pumps, motors, or valves** using custom objects.
- Encapsulate related data and methods for **cleaner code reuse**.
- Use in **project libraries** to centralize logic (e.g., calculations, validations).

Example Usage

```
p1 = Pump("TransferPump1", 1450)
print p1.name     # Output: TransferPump1
print p1.rpm      # Output: 1450
```

Use Case: Monitoring Pump RPMs in a Gateway Timer Script

You want to **track several pumps** and log a warning if any pump's RPM drops below its operational threshold. Using a class makes it easy to organize the data and logic.

Step 1: Define the Pump Class in a Project Script

Path: Project Library > scripting > pumputils

```
# pumputils.py

class Pump:
  def __init__(self, name, rpmTag, minRpm):
    self.name = name
    self.rpmTag = rpmTag
    self.minRpm = minRpm
    self.rpm = 0

  def readRpm(self):
    result = system.tag.readBlocking([self.rpmTag])[0]
    if result.quality.isGood():
      self.rpm = result.value
    else:
      raise Exception("Bad tag quality for " + self.name)

  def isRunningBelowMinimum(self):
    return self.rpm < self.minRpm
```

Step 2: Use It in a Gateway Timer Script

```
import pumputils
logger = system.util.getLogger("PumpMonitor")

pumps = [
  pumputils.Pump("Pump A", "[Site A]Motors/Motor 1/Speed", 1200),
  pumputils.Pump("Pump B", "[Site A]Motors/Motor 2/Speed", 1000)
]

for pump in pumps:
  try:
    pump.readRpm()
    if pump.isRunningBelowMinimum():
      logger.warn(
          pump.name + " running below threshold: " +
          str(pump.rpm) + " RPM"
          )
    else:
      logger.info(pump.name + " is OK: " + str(pump.rpm) + " RPM")
  except Exception as e:
    logger.error("Error with " + pump.name + ": " + str(e))
```

Benefits in Context

- Easy to expand by adding methods like logStatus(), reset(), or calculate Efficiency().
- Keeps logic **organized and reusable** for multiple pumps or other devices.
- Great for Gateway scripts that need to **monitor**, **diagnose**, or **report** device status.

14.2 Adding Methods to Your Classes

In Jython, **methods** are functions defined inside a class that operate on the object's data. In Ignition, this is especially helpful for encapsulating tag logic, control commands, or device behaviors, making your code **organized**, **reusable**, and **easier to maintain**.

Example: Define the Motor Class in a Project Script Module

In the **Project Library**, create a script module called devices

Add this code inside:

```
# devices.py

class Motor:
    def __init__(self, tagPath):
        self.tagPath = tagPath

    def start(self):
        system.tag.writeBlocking([self.tagPath + "/Start"], [1])

    def stop(self):
        system.tag.writeBlocking([self.tagPath + "/Start"], [0])
```

This class is now available across your entire project.

What Each Part Does:

class Motor:

- Declares a new class named Motor. This is a *template* for any motor you want to control.

def __init__(self, tagPath):

- This is the **constructor** method. It runs automatically when you create a new Motor object.
- self.tagPath = tagPath saves the full base tag path for later use (e.g., [Site A]Motors/Motor1).

def start(self):

- This is a **method** (function inside the class) that writes 1 to the motor's /Start tag — telling it to turn on.

def stop(self):

- This writes 0 to the /Start tag — turning the motor off.

Call the Class from a Button (Vision or Perspective)

```
from devices import Motor

# Define the motor
m1 = Motor("[Site A]Motors/Motor 1")

# Start the motor
m1.start()
```

This creates an instance of the Motor class named m1.

- The constructor stores the tag path "[Site A]Motors/Motor 1" inside the object.
- Now m1 has access to the start() and stop() methods that operate on that path.

Sample Exercises

Exercise 1: Define a Simple Class and Create an Object

Objective:

· Create a Device class with a name and a method to print its status.

Script:

```
class Device:
def __init__(self, name):
self.name = name

def report(self):
print self.name + " is operational."

d = Device("Pump A")
d.report()
```

What You Learn: How to define a class, create an object, and call a method in Jython.

Exercise 2: Use Object Properties to Store Tag Values

Objective:

· Store a device's tag value in an object attribute.

Script:

```
class Sensor:
def __init__(self, tagPath):
self.tagPath = tagPath
self.value = system.tag.readBlocking([tagPath])[0].value

def report(self):
print "Sensor at", self.tagPath, "has value:", self.value

s = Sensor("[default]Boiler/Pressure")
s.report()
```

What You Learn: How to use a class to encapsulate tag information and behavior.

Exercise 4: Add a Method That Returns a Computed Value

Objective:

· Add a method that calculates total runtime based on speed.

Script:

```
class Device:
def __init__(self, name, hours, speed):
self.name = name
self.hours = hours
self.speed = speed

def energyUsed(self):
return self.hours * self.speed

d = Device("Fan 1", 10, 1500)
print "Energy Used:", d.energyUsed()
```

What You Learn: How to create a method that returns a value based on internal object state.

Exercise 5: Simulate a Real-World Object with Tag Integration

Objective:

- Build a Tank class that reads live level and prints alert if overfilled.

Script:

```
class Tank:
def __init__(self, name, tagPath):
self.name = name
self.level = system.tag.readBlocking([tagPath])[0].value

def check(self):
if self.level > 90:
print self.name + " is over 90% full!"
else:
print self.name + " level is normal."

t = Tank("Storage Tank 1", "[Site A]Tank1/Level")
t.check()
```

What You Learn: How to combine class structure with live system data for monitoring logic.

15

Chapter 15: Methods and Encapsulation

Methods and encapsulation in Ignition scripting are key principles of object–oriented programming. Methods are functions defined within a class that operate on its data, while encapsulation keeps internal variables and logic hidden from outside access. This promotes modular, maintainable code by exposing only what's necessary through controlled interfaces. Using methods to group related behavior and encapsulating data helps reduce errors and makes complex Ignition scripts easier to manage, reuse, and debug across automation systems.

15.1 Defining Instance Methods

Instance methods are functions defined inside a class that act on the data stored within that specific object (or "instance"). In Ignition, instance methods are especially valuable when working with **tag-based devices**, because they allow you to encapsulate device behavior in reusable, structured logic.

Example: Light Device with On/Off Methods

```
class Light:
    def __init__(self, tagPath):
        self.tagPath = tagPath

    def turnOn(self):
        system.tag.writeBlocking([self.tagPath], [1])

    def turnOff(self):
        system.tag.writeBlocking([self.tagPath], [0])
```

- ___init___() sets the tag path of the light.
- turnOn() writes a value of 1 to turn the light on.
- turnOff() writes a 0 to turn it off.

How to Use It

```
lobbyLight = Light("[Site A]Lights/Lobby")
lobbyLight.turnOn()
```

- The object lobbyLight knows which tag to control.
- Its turnOn() and turnOff() methods are tied to that specific tag path.

Why Use Instance Methods?

- Avoid repeating tag paths or write logic in every script.
- Make device interactions cleaner and more intuitive (e.g., light.turnOff() instead of writing tags manually).
- Makes project scripts more modular, reusable, and testable.

15.2 Access Modifiers: Public and Private

In Jython, unlike Java, there's no enforced access control (like private or protected). However, developers follow **naming conventions** to indicate whether variables or methods are intended for **internal (private)** use or **external (public)** access.

Convention Guidelines:

- Names **without an underscore** are considered **public** — intended for external use.
- Names **starting with a single underscore (_)** are considered **private** — intended for internal logic only.
- Names with **double underscores** (e.g., __var) invoke name mangling but are rarely used in Ignition scripting.

Example: Valve with Public and Private Members

```
class Valve:
   def __init__(self, name):
      self.name = name        # Public
      self._state = "Closed"    # Intended to be private

   def open(self):
      self._state = "Open"
```

- self.name is accessible and expected to be used externally (e.g., in logs or UI).
- self._state is used internally to track status and should not be accessed directly outside the class.

Why This Matters in Ignition

- Helps teams avoid misusing internal logic in shared project scripts.
- Improves readability, clarity, and safety in large automation projects.
- Encourages encapsulation when modeling devices or process logic.

Even though Jython won't block access to _state, using this convention keeps your code **predictable** and **maintainable**.

15.3 Getters and Setters

Getter and setter methods provide controlled access to internal object attributes. Rather than exposing variables directly, these methods allow you to **validate**, **transform**, or **restrict** how values are read or written — which is especially useful in Ignition for managing user roles, tag wrappers, or session properties.

Example: Operator Role Management

```
class Operator:
  def __init__(self):
    self._role = None

  def setRole(self, role):
    if role in ["admin", "user", "viewer"]:
      self._role = role

  def getRole(self):
    return self._role
```

- setRole() enforces that only approved role names are accepted.
- getRole() retrieves the current role value.
- The internal _role variable remains private and protected from bad data.

Why Use Getters and Setters in Ignition

- Prevent invalid values (e.g., unknown user roles, out-of-range numbers)
- Transform inputs or apply logic (e.g., trimming, formatting)
- Use in **Perspective session startup scripts**, where roles or settings must be sanitized
- Wrap tag access in classes while applying read/write rules

Example Use in Perspective

```
user = Operator()
user.setRole("admin")
print user.getRole()  # Output: admin
```

· This pattern is especially useful when building **session-based user controls**, **secure configuration classes**, or **tag access layers** with validation.

15.4 Method Overloading

Jython, unlike Java, **does not support method overloading** by defining multiple methods with the same name and different argument signatures. Instead, you can simulate overloading behavior using **default parameter values**, ***args/**kwargs**, or conditional logic inside the method.

Example: Simulated Overloading with Default Values

```
class Alert:
  def notify(self, msg, level="info"):
    if level == "critical":
      system.gui.warningBox(msg)
    else:
      print msg
```

· notify() accepts one required argument (msg) and one optional argument (level).
· If level is "critical", it shows a warning box in the Vision Client.
· Otherwise, it prints the message to the console.

Why This Matters in Ignition

- Helps simplify script APIs for user-defined classes
- Keeps logic flexible without duplicating method names
- Useful in Vision or Perspective for **alert handlers**, **device control**, or **logging utilities**

Example Usage

```
a = Alert()
a.notify("System is normal")          # Prints message
a.notify("Pump failure!", level="critical")   # Shows warning popup
```

You can also inspect arguments dynamically using *args if needed:

```
def notify(self, *args):
    if len(args) == 1:
        print args[0]
    elif len(args) == 2:
        msg, level = args
        if level == "critical":
            system.gui.warningBox(msg)
        else:
            print msg
```

Reusable Pattern: Flexible DeviceController Class

- **Goal:** Create a single class that handles **start/stop**, accepts **optional logging**, and supports both **explicit** and **default behavior** using manual overloading logic.

Project Script Module: deviceutils

```
# deviceutils.py

class DeviceController:
    def __init__(self, basePath, logger=None):
        self.basePath = basePath
        self.logger = logger if logger else system.util.getLogger("DeviceController")

    def command(self, action="start", level="info"):
        tagPath = self.basePath + "/Start"

        try:
            if action.lower() == "start":
                system.tag.writeBlocking([tagPath], [1])
                self._log("Started " + self.basePath, level)

            elif action.lower() == "stop":
                system.tag.writeBlocking([tagPath], [0])
                self._log("Stopped " + self.basePath, level)

            else:
                self._log("Unknown action: " + action, "warn")

        except Exception as e:
            self._log("Error during action '" + action + "': " + str(e), "error")
```

class DeviceController:

- Defines a class named DeviceController. Each object created from this class will control a specific device based on a tag path.

__init__(self, basePath, logger=None)

- Purpose: Initializes the controller with a base tag path.
- basePath: The root path of the device, like [Site A]Motors/Motor 1.
- logger: Optional. If not provided, it creates a logger named "DeviceController" using Ignition's system.util.getLogger().

  For example, basePath + "/Start" becomes [Site A]Motors/Motor 1/Start

```
def _log(self, msg, level):
  if level == "debug":
    self.logger.debug(msg)
  elif level == "info":
    self.logger.info(msg)
  elif level == "warn":
    self.logger.warn(msg)
  elif level == "error":
    self.logger.error(msg)
  else:
    self.logger.info(msg)
```

Purpose of _log(self, msg, level)

- This method is a **private helper function** (by naming convention, because it starts with an underscore) used to send log messages to the **Ignition system log**, based on a specified **severity level**.

- It simplifies and centralizes logging so that your start() and stop() methods don't have to repeat if/else logic to choose the correct log method.

def _log(self, msg, level):

- Accepts a log message (msg)
- Accepts a log level string (level) such as "debug", "info", etc.
- Uses self.logger, which was defined in the constructor (___init___) as the logger instance (via system.util.getLogger())

Example Usage in a Button Script for Start Button

```
from deviceutils import DeviceController

motor = DeviceController("[Site A]Motors/Motor 1")
motor.start("debug")  # Starts and logs at debug level
```

- **Imports** the DeviceController class from your shared project script module deviceutils.

Creates a motor object that is tied to the tag path:

- [Site A]Motors/Motor 1
- Calls the start() method, which:
- Writes 1 to the tag [Site A]Motors/Motor 1/Start
- Logs the action using system.util.getLogger("DeviceController") at the "debug" level

Use Case: This script would be placed on a **Start button** in a Vision or

Perspective view. When pressed, it starts the motor and logs a debug message, useful during testing or diagnostics.

Example Usage in a Button Script for Stop Button

```
from deviceutils import DeviceController

motor = DeviceController("[Site A]Motors/Motor 1")
motor.stop("info")   # Stops with info-level logging
```

- Same import and object creation as the Start button
- Calls the stop() method, which:
- Writes 1 to the tag [Site A]Motors/Motor 1/Stop
- Logs the action at the "info" level (normal operational log)

Use Case: This script would be placed on a **Stop button**, allowing an operator to safely stop the motor and record the action in the system log.

Notes:

- Both buttons **instantiate the same class** with the device's base tag path.
- **Start and Stop use different Boolean tags** under that base path.
- The class handles **logging, tag writing**, and optional log severity.

This setup keeps your **UI scripts clean** while letting you control logging levels and logic from a **central class**, which is especially scalable in large systems with many motors or devices.

15.5 The self Keyword and Object Identity

In Jython (and Python), the self keyword is used to refer to the **current instance of a class**. It allows methods to **access and modify attributes and call other methods** within the same object. Think of self as the object's personal reference to itself.

Example: A Simple Counter

```
class Counter:
  def __init__(self):
    self.value = 0

  def increment(self):
    self.value += 1
    print self.value
```

- self.value = 0: initializes an attribute named value that belongs to the specific object.
- self.value += 1: updates that specific object's value.
- print self.value: displays the updated value.

What Happens When You Use It

```
c1 = Counter()
c2 = Counter()

c1.increment() # Output: 1
c2.increment() # Output: 1
c1.increment() # Output: 2
```

- c1 and c2 are **separate objects**.
- Each one keeps its own **state** (value), which is tracked through self.

Why This Matters in Ignition

Using self ensures that:

- Each device, session, or UI component maintains its own **independent behavior**
- You can safely reuse the same class across **multiple components**, tag paths, or user sessions without overlap
- Your logic is **modular** and **object-specific**

This is especially useful when simulating devices, managing multi-user workflows in Perspective, or handling multiple control panels in Vision.

Sample Exercises

Exercise 1: Create a Class with Public Methods

Objective:

- Define a class with methods that can be called from the outside.

Script:

```
class Fan:
def __init__(self, name):
self.name = name
self.running = False

def start(self):
self.running = True
print self.name + " started."

def stop(self):
self.running = False
print self.name + " stopped."

f = Fan("Cooling Fan A")
f.start()
f.stop()
```

What You Learn: How to use public methods to control internal object state.

Exercise 2: Use Internal Variables with Encapsulation

Objective:

- Access and modify internal data using getter and setter methods.

Script:

```
class Valve:
def __init__(self):
self.__position = 0 # Private attribute

def setPosition(self, pos):
if 0 <= pos <= 100:
self.__position = pos
else:
print "Invalid position."

def getPosition(self):
return self.__position

v = Valve()
v.setPosition(75)
print "Valve position is:", v.getPosition()
```

What You Learn: How to encapsulate internal data and expose it through safe public methods.

Exercise 3: Apply Encapsulation with Tag Integration

Objective:

· Encapsulate tag read/write logic in class methods.

Script:

```
class Motor:
def __init__(self, tagPath):
self.__tagPath = tagPath

def getSpeed(self):
return system.tag.readBlocking([self.__tagPath])[0].value

def setSpeed(self, rpm):
system.tag.writeBlocking([self.__tagPath], [rpm])

m = Motor("[default]Motor1/Speed")
print "Speed:", m.getSpeed()
m.setSpeed(1200)
```

What You Learn: How to abstract tag interaction through class methods.

Exercise 4: Use Helper Methods Inside a Class

Objective:

· Break a class's logic into private and public methods.

Script:

```
class Sensor:
def __init__(self, name, value):
self.name = name
self.__value = value

def __alert(self):
print self.name + " value out of range!"

def check(self):
if self.__value > 100:
self.__alert()
else:
print self.name + " is within range."

s = Sensor("Pressure Sensor", 105)
s.check()
```

What You Learn: How to organize logic by separating internal helper methods from public methods.

Exercise 5: Build an Object with Controlled State Updates

Objective:

- Create a class that modifies internal values only through validation logic.

Script:

```
class Tank:
def __init__(self, name):
self.name = name
self._level = 0

def fill(self, amount):
if amount > 0:
self._level += amount
print self.name + " filled by", amount
else:
print "Invalid fill amount."

def getLevel(self):
return self._level

t = Tank("Tank A")
t.fill(20)
print "Current level:", t.getLevel()
```

What You Learn: How to enforce rules and protect object state through encapsulated methods.

16

Chapter 16: Inheritance and Polymorphism

Inheritance and polymorphism in Ignition scripting allow you to build flexible, reusable class hierarchies. Inheritance enables a class to derive behavior and attributes from a parent class, reducing redundancy and promoting code reuse. Polymorphism allows objects from different classes to be treated the same if they share a common interface, enabling consistent interaction across varying types. These object-oriented principles support scalable and organized scripting, especially in complex Ignition projects that model equipment, alarms, or user-defined behaviors.

16.1 Understanding Inheritance

Inheritance is an object-oriented feature that allows one class (called a *child* or *subclass*) to **reuse the properties and methods** of another class (called a *parent* or *superclass*). In Ignition, this is especially useful for modeling devices that share common behaviors — such as logging, tag handling, or state control — while allowing each device type to define its own specific actions.

Example: Base Device Class and Motor Subclass

```
class Device:
    def __init__(self, name):
        self.name = name

    def logStatus(self):
        print self.name + " status logged."

class Motor(Device):
    def start(self):
        print self.name + " motor started."
```

Device is the **parent class** that defines shared behavior, such as name and logStatus().

Motor is a child class that:

- Inherits __init__() and logStatus() from Device
- Adds its own method, start(), specific to motors

Why Use Inheritance in Ignition?

- Reduces duplicate code across multiple device types (motors, valves, lights)
- Centralizes shared functionality (logging, validation, status checks)
- Makes large projects more maintainable and scalable
- Ideal for **script modules** when modeling real-world devices in a structured way

16.2 Overriding Methods for Custom Behavior

When a child class **inherits** a method from a parent class, it can also **override** that method by redefining it. This lets you **customize the behavior** of the inherited method without changing the parent class — ideal when different device types need specialized logic while still fitting into a shared structure.

Example: Overriding logStatus() in a Sensor Class

```
class Sensor(Device):
    def logStatus(self):
        print self.name + ": Sensor reading stored."
```

- The Sensor class overrides logStatus(), replacing the version defined in the Device class.
- Now, when logStatus() is called on a Sensor object, it executes the **custom version**.

Demonstration:

```
s = Sensor("TempSensor1")
s.logStatus()  # Output: TempSensor1: Sensor reading stored.
```

Even though Sensor inherits from Device, it provides its own logging logic. This is a powerful tool when managing multiple device types in Ignition that behave similarly but not identically.

Why It Matters in Ignition

- Lets you **standardize interfaces** while customizing behavior (e.g., start(), logStatus(), checkAlarms()).
- Makes your code **easier to maintain** — changes to common logic go in the base class, while custom cases stay isolated.
- Useful for projects with multiple equipment models, device families, or control types.

16.3 Using super() to Extend Parent Methods

When a child class **overrides** a method but still wants to use the **parent version**, it can call it using super(). This is helpful when you want to **extend behavior rather than replace it** — for example, logging, setup, or validation logic defined in a base class.

Example: Extending logStatus() Before Starting a Motor

```
class Motor(Device):
  def start(self):
    super(Motor, self).logStatus()
    print self.name + " motor started."
```

- super(Motor, self).logStatus() calls the logStatus() method from the parent Device class.
- The print self.name + " motor started." line adds custom behavior **after** the inherited action.
- The start() method now logs **and** starts the motor.

Example Usage:

```
m = Motor("Pump A")
m.start()
```

Output:

```
Pump A status logged.
Pump A motor started.
```

Why Use super() in Ignition

- Allows you to **inject common functionality** (like logging or validation) without repeating code

- Supports **safe overrides**, so changes in the parent class still take effect
- Keeps logic **modular** and **traceable** — great for scripting control logic across multiple device types

16.4 Polymorphism: One Interface, Many Behaviors

Polymorphism means different object types can share the same interface (i.e., method names), but each defines **its own unique behavior**. In Jython and Ignition scripting, this lets you write code that **works generically**, even when the underlying logic varies per object type.

Example: Shared Method, Different Implementations

```
devices = [Sensor("S1"), Motor("M1")]

for d in devices:
    d.logStatus()
```

- Both Sensor and Motor classes have a logStatus() method.
- The loop doesn't care **what kind** of object d is — it just calls logStatus().
- Each object handles the method **in its own way,** thanks to **method overriding**.

Why Polymorphism Matters in Ignition

- **Simplifies your logic**: Write one loop to handle devices of different types.
- **Supports flexible architectures**: Add new device classes without rewriting your logic.

Ideal for:

- **Dynamic dashboards** (update based on device class)
- **Batch control scripts** (execute based on interface, not object type)
- **Centralized logging, validation, or diagnostics**

16.5 Practical Use in Ignition Projects

Using classes, inheritance, and polymorphism in Ignition scripting helps you **build scalable, maintainable, and reusable code** — especially when working with tags, devices, or data processing.

Common Use Cases

Device Abstraction

- Create a base class like Device to hold shared logic (e.g., name, logging, tag writes), and extend it for specific components like Motor, Sensor, or Valve.

Reusability

- Place shared methods — like logStatus(), getAlarmState(), or writeCommand() — in the parent class to avoid repeating logic.

Polymorphism for Simplified Logic

- Treat different objects the same in your control loops or UI scripts by using consistent method names like read(), start(), or log().

Gateway Event Scripting

- Use class hierarchies to create flexible, testable **data handlers**, **alarm processors**, or **batch controllers**.

Example: Tag Reader with Inheritance

```
class TagReader:
  def read(self, path):
    return system.tag.readBlocking([path])[0].value

class AveragingReader(TagReader):
  def read(self, paths):
    values = [system.tag.readBlocking([p])[0].value for p in paths]
    return sum(values) / len(values)
```

- TagReader is a **base class** that reads a single tag.
- AveragingReader is a **subclass** that overrides read() to handle **multiple tags**, returning their average.

```
single = TagReader()
print single.read("[Site A]Tank/Level")

multi = AveragingReader()
avg = multi.read(["[Site A]Tank/Level1", "[Site A]Tank/Level2"])
print "Average:", avg
```

Why It Works Well in Ignition

- Keeps gateway scripts organized
- Reduces code duplication across projects
- Makes Perspective and Vision event scripts **cleaner** and **more testable**
- Encourages **modular development**, especially on teams

Sample Exercises

Exercise 1: Create a Base Class and a Subclass

Objective:

- Use inheritance to create a specialized device type.

Script:

```
class Device:
def __init__(self, name):
self.name = name

def report(self):
print self.name + " is a generic device."

class Pump(Device):
def report(self):
print self.name + " is a pump device."

d1 = Device("Device A")
d2 = Pump("Pump B")

d1.report()
d2.report()
```

What You Learn: How to create a base class and override its method in a subclass.

Exercise 2: Use super() to Extend Base Class Behavior

Objective:

· Enhance inherited methods while preserving base functionality.

Script:

```
class Motor:
def __init__(self, name):
self.name = name

def start(self):
print self.name + " is starting..."

class VFD(Motor):
def start(self):
super(VFD, self).start()
print self.name + " is ramping up speed with VFD."

m = VFD("Main Motor")
m.start()
```

What You Learn: How to use super() to call parent methods before extending them.

Exercise 3: Create a Polymorphic Report System

Objective:

· Use polymorphism to call the same method on different object types.

Script:

```
class Sensor:
def __init__(self, name):
self.name = name

def read(self):
print self.name + ": generic sensor reading."

class TempSensor(Sensor):
def read(self):
print self.name + ": temperature = 72.4°F"

class PressureSensor(Sensor):
def read(self):
print self.name + ": pressure = 145 psi"

sensors = [TempSensor("T1"), PressureSensor("P1"), Sensor("S3")]

for s in sensors:
s.read()
```

What You Learn: How polymorphism enables uniform access to varied behavior.

Exercise 4: Inherit From a Base Class That Handles Tags

Objective:

· Build tag-aware subclasses using a common parent.

Script:

```
class TagDevice:
def __init__(self, tagPath):
self.tagPath = tagPath

def getValue(self):
return system.tag.readBlocking([self.tagPath])[0].value

class FlowSensor(TagDevice):
def report(self):
print "Flow rate:", self.getValue()

f = FlowSensor("[default]Flow/Rate")
f.report()
```

What You Learn: How to reuse tag logic in multiple subclasses.

Exercise 5: Override Initialization in Subclasses

Objective:

· Customize the ___init___ method in derived classes.

Script:

```
class Machine:
def __init__(self, name):
self.name = name
print self.name + " registered."

class Mixer(Machine):
def __init__(self, name, rpm):
super(Mixer, self).__init__(name)
self.rpm = rpm

def showRPM(self):
print self.name + " running at " + str(self.rpm) + " RPM"

m = Mixer("Batch Mixer", 1450)
m.showRPM()
```

What You Learn: How to customize initialization in subclasses while retaining base logic.

17

Chapter 17: Class and Static Methods

Class and static methods in Ignition scripting provide alternative ways to define functionality within classes that don't rely on instance-specific data. Class methods, marked with @classmethod, receive the class itself as the first argument and are useful for factory patterns or class-wide operations. Static methods, marked with @staticmethod, operate independently of both class and instance, ideal for utility functions grouped logically within a class. These methods support organized, reusable code structures and are helpful when scripting modular logic in larger Ignition projects.

17.1 Understanding Class Variables

Class variables are variables that are shared by **all instances** of a class. Unlike instance variables (which are tied to a specific object via self), class variables are tied to the class itself and defined **outside of any method**, typically right under the class name.

Example: Counting Object Instances

```
class Counter:
    count = 0  # This is a class variable

    def __init__(self):
        Counter.count += 1
```

- count is a **class variable**.
- Every time a new Counter object is created, the class variable count is incremented.
- This allows you to **track the number of objects created** across your entire script.

Use in Ignition

You might use class variables to:

- Count how many **scripts have executed**
- Track **how many devices were instantiated**
- Accumulate **total errors or alarm events**

214

- Share a **global constant** (e.g., MAX_DEVICES = 10)

Example Usage:

```
c1 = Counter()
c2 = Counter()
c3 = Counter()

print Counter.count  # Output: 3
```

All three objects update the same Counter.count, because it belongs to the class — not the instance.

Why It Matters in Ignition

- **Ideal for global counters**, without needing tag memory or gateway variables
- Useful in **testing, logging, or diagnostics**
- Makes it easy to build behavior that reflects **overall system state**, not just individual object state

17.2 Creating Class Methods with @classmethod

A **class method** is a method that operates on the **class itself**, rather than on an instance of the class. It uses the @classmethod decorator and takes cls as the first parameter instead of self.

This is useful when you want to:

- Access or modify class variables
- Create objects using custom logic

· Register global mappings or actions used across your project

Example: Role Registry

```
class Operator:
    roles = [] # Class-level list shared by all Operator instances

    @classmethod
    def addRole(cls, role):
        cls.roles.append(role)
```

· roles is a **class variable**, shared across all Operator objects.
· addRole() is a **class method** that appends a new role to that shared list.
· The cls keyword refers to the class Operator, not a specific object.

Example Usage

```
Operator.addRole("admin")
Operator.addRole("viewer")

print Operator.roles
# Output: ['admin', 'viewer']
```

This allows you to maintain a **shared list of user roles** across your project.

Why It Matters in Ignition

· Use @classmethod in **Gateway Event Scripts** to update system-wide configs like:

- role permissions
- device type mappings
- global logging registries
- Supports flexible design without needing global variables or persistent tags

17.3 Creating Static Methods with @staticmethod

A **static method** is a method that belongs to a class but doesn't access or modify the class (cls) or an instance (self). It behaves like a **regular function**, but is placed inside a class for **organizational clarity**.

Use static methods when you want to:

- Group related logic under a common class (like utilities, device math, or alarm tools)
- Perform calculations, formatting, or conversions without needing class context

Example: Scaling a Value

```
class MathHelper:
  @staticmethod
  def scaleValue(value, factor):
    return value * factor
```

- @staticmethod indicates this function doesn't use self or cls.
- scaleValue() just multiplies value by factor — a **pure utility function**.

Example Usage

```
print MathHelper.scaleValue(10, 1.5)
# Output: 15.0
```

No object of MathHelper is needed — it's simply called on the class itself.

Why Static Methods Matter in Ignition

Great for reusable logic like:

- scaling sensor values
- unit conversions
- tag name formatting
- alarm calculations
- Keeps utility code **organized inside your class** instead of floating around your script modules
- Perfect for **project libraries** that support Perspective or Gateway scripts

17.4 Choosing Between Instance, Class, and Static Methods

Instance Methods

- Use self
- Access or modify object-level attributes
- Ideal for defining device behavior like start(), stop(), or logStatus()

Class Methods

- Use @classmethod and cls
- Modify or interact with class-level data
- Useful for shared configuration, tracking instances, or building alternate constructors

Static Methods

- Use @staticmethod
- Don't use self or cls
- Great for **utility functions** such as scaling, validation, formatting, or conversions

In Ignition Projects

- Use **instance methods** for per-device logic (e.g., controlling motors or sensors)
- Use **class methods** for maintaining global lists, role mappings, or counters
- Use **static methods** for clean, organized utility logic (e.g., formatting tag paths, unit conversions)

Sample Exercises

Exercise 1: Define a Static Method for Utility Logic

Objective:

- Create a method that doesn't access instance or class attributes.

Script:

```
class MathTools:
@staticmethod
def rpmToHz(rpm):
return rpm / 60.0

print "60 RPM =", MathTools.rpmToHz(60), "Hz"
```

What You Learn: How to define and use @staticmethod for general-purpose logic.

Exercise 2: Use a Static Method for Alarm Message Formatting

Objective:

· Centralize formatting logic for alarm messages.

Script:

```
class AlarmHelper:
@staticmethod
def formatMessage(device, status):
return "[ALERT] {} is in '{}' state.".format(device, status)

msg = AlarmHelper.formatMessage("Pump A", "Fault")
print msg
```

What You Learn: How to use static methods to encapsulate shared string logic.

Exercise 3: Create a Class Method to Track Instances

Objective:

· Use @classmethod to maintain a shared counter across all objects.

Script:

```
class Sensor:
count = 0

def __init__(self, name):
self.name = name
Sensor.count += 1

@classmethod
def getSensorCount(cls):
return cls.count

s1 = Sensor("S1")
s2 = Sensor("S2")

print "Total sensors created:", Sensor.getSensorCount()
```

What You Learn: How @classmethod can access and modify class-level data.

Exercise 4: Create a Factory Method Using a Class Method

Objective:

· Use a class method to create preconfigured objects.

Script:

```
class Motor:
def __init__(self, name, rpm):
self.name = name
self.rpm = rpm

@classmethod
def standardMotor(cls):
return cls("Standard Motor", 1750)

m = Motor.standardMotor()
print m.name, "at", m.rpm, "RPM"
```

What You Learn: How class methods can serve as alternative constructors.

Exercise 5: Mix Static and Class Methods in a Tag-Aware Class

Objective:

· Create a tag–driven device with utility logic as static methods.

Script:

```
class Device:
deviceCount = 0

def __init__(self, tagPath):
self.tagPath = tagPath
Device.deviceCount += 1

@staticmethod
def statusToText(code):
return {0: "Stopped", 1: "Running", 2: "Fault"}.get(code, "Unknown")

@classmethod
def getDeviceCount(cls):
return cls.deviceCount

d = Device("[default]Motor1/Status")
print "Status:", Device.statusToText(1)
print "Devices created:", Device.getDeviceCount()
```

What You Learn: How to combine static utility logic with class-level counters in a reusable structure.

18

Chapter 18: Magic Methods and Overloading

Magic methods and overloading in Ignition scripting allow classes to define custom behavior for built-in Python operations. Magic methods like ___init___, ___str___, and ___add___ enable you to control how objects are created, displayed, or interact with operators. Overloading these methods allows objects to behave intuitively, such as using + to combine custom types. This enhances the flexibility and readability of your code, making classes feel more natural to use and extending Python's functionality within Ignition's scripting environment.

18.1 Introduction to Magic Methods (__init__, __str__, etc.)

Magic methods (also known as **dunder methods**, short for "double underscore") are special built-in method names in Python that let you define how your objects behave in common situations — like creation, comparison, printing, and more.

These methods help make your classes feel **natural and intuitive**, especially when debugging, logging, or managing device objects in Ignition.

Common Magic Methods in Ignition Scripting

__init__(self, ...)

- Called when a new object is created (your **constructor**).
- Used to initialize instance attributes.

__str__(self)

- Defines how your object is represented as a string (e.g., in logs or print).
- Useful for **debugging, scripting consoles, or logging to system.util.ge tLogger()**.

__len__(self)

- Allows your object to respond to len(obj) — useful when your class wraps collections or datasets.

__eq__(self, other)

- Defines how two objects are compared with ==.
- Ideal for comparing device names, states, or configurations.

Example: Custom String Representation

```
class Sensor:
  def __init__(self, name, value):
    self.name = name
    self.value = value

  def __str__(self):
    return "Sensor %s: %.2f" % (self.name, self.value)
```

· Now, when you print or log a Sensor object, it uses your custom format:

```
s = Sensor("Flow", 12.78)
print str(s)  # Output: Sensor Flow: 12.78
```

· Without ___str___(), it would print something like <Sensor object at 0x3ffaf> — not helpful in a system log or UI.

Why Magic Methods Matter in Ignition

· Improve **readability** in logs and print statements (especially in system.ut il.getLogger())
· Make your objects **easier to work with** in Gateway and Vision scripting
· Enable meaningful comparisons, sizes, and behavior for **custom tag wrappers**, **device classes**, and **scripted UI elements**

18.2 Customizing Object Output with __str__ and __repr__

In Jython (and Python), you can define two special magic methods to control how your objects display when logged or printed:

- __str__() – controls the human-readable output, such as what appears in print statements, Vision/Perspective bindings, or logs.
- __repr__() – controls the developer/debugging view, such as what's shown in the Script Console or error traces.

Defining both methods helps make your custom classes more transparent, testable, and debug-friendly — especially in complex Ignition projects.

Example: A Sensor Class with Both Methods

```
class Sensor:
  def __init__(self, name, value):
    self.name = name
    self.value = value

  def __str__(self):
    return "Sensor %s: %.2f" % (self.name, self.value)

  def __repr__(self):
    return "<Sensor name='%s' value=%.2f>" % (self.name, self.value)
```

Example Usage in Ignition

```
s = Sensor("Flow", 12.78)

print s      # Calls __str__ → Sensor Flow: 12.78
s            # Typing this alone in the Script Console calls __repr__
```

Why This Is Useful in Ignition

- Makes your project library objects **easier to debug**
- Improves clarity when inspecting return values in the **Script Console**
- Helps track and log object state in **Gateway scripts**, **Perspective logs**, or **custom device models**

18.3 Operator Overloading with Custom Classes

Operator overloading allows you to define how standard operators like +, -, *, ==, or > behave when used with **your custom objects**. This makes your classes behave more naturally in expressions and calculations — perfect for modeling things like tag readings, durations, or energy totals in Ignition.

Example: Overloading + for a Reading Class

```
class Reading:
    def __init__(self, value):
        self.value = value

    def __add__(self, other):
        return Reading(self.value + other.value)
```

- ___add___ is a **magic method** that defines what happens when you use the + operator.

· It takes other as the second object and returns a new Reading with the combined value.

Usage

```
r1 = Reading(5)
r2 = Reading(10)
total = r1 + r2
print total.value  # Output: 15
```

· Now you can use + just like you would with numbers — but behind the scenes, your custom logic handles the operation.

Why This Matters in Ignition

· Makes your device or data model objects more **intuitive** to use

Great for:

· **Summing sensor values**
· **Combining durations**
· **Building totals across loops** (e.g., runtime, flow, pressure)
· Keeps your scripting **cleaner and more readable**, especially when objects represent meaningful data types

18.4 Comparison Methods (__eq__, __lt__, etc.)

Python (and Jython) allows you to define how your objects behave when compared using operators like ==, <, or >. These are called **comparison**

magic methods, and they let your custom classes be used in **sorting**, **filtering**, and **conditional logic** — just like built-in types.

Example: Define Equality with __eq__

```
def __eq__(self, other):
  return self.name == other.name and self.value == other.value
```

- This method checks if **two objects** are equal by comparing their internal attributes.
- You use this when determining if two sensors or devices **represent the same state**.
- Additional Comparison Methods

Example: Sensor Comparison with __eq__

```
class Sensor:
  def __init__(self, name, value):
    self.name = name
    self.value = value

  def __eq__(self, other):
    if isinstance(other, Sensor):
      return self.name == other.name and self.value == other.value
    return False

  def __str__(self):
    return "Sensor(%s: %.2f)" % (self.name, self.value)
```

Code Explanation:

Created as a script in a project script named "MagicMethods"

class Sensor:

- Defines a new class called Sensor. Each Sensor object will hold data like a name and a numeric value (e.g., from a tank level or pressure tag).

def __init__(self, name, value):

self.name = name

self.value = value

- This is the **constructor** (___init___) — it runs when you create a new Sensor object.
- It assigns name and value to the object's internal state using self.

def __eq__(self, other):

if isinstance(other, Sensor):

return self.name == other.name and self.value == other.value

return False

- This defines **how equality (==) is evaluated** between two Sensor objects.
- isinstance(other, Sensor) makes sure the object being compared is also a Sensor. This prevents crashes if someone tries to compare a sensor to something else.

Then it compares:

- self.name == other.name
- self.value == other.value

Returns True only if both match — otherwise returns False.

def __str__(self):

return "Sensor(%s: %.2f)" % (self.name, self.value)

- This controls what gets shown when the object is printed or logged.
- %s is a placeholder for a string (self.name), and %.2f formats the value as a float with two decimal places.

Example in Ignition's Script Console

```
s1 = Sensor("Tank1", 82.5)
s2 = Sensor("Tank1", 82.5)
s3 = Sensor("Tank2", 90)

print s1 == s2   # True (same name and value)
print s1 == s3   # False
print str(s1)    # Sensor(Tank1: 82.50)
```

Output

```
>>>
True
False
Sensor(Tank1: 82.50)
>>>
```

You can also implement these to support full ordering and sorting:

- ___lt___(self, other) → less than (<)
- ___gt___(self, other) → greater than (>)
- ___le___(self, other) → less than or equal (<=)
- ___ge___(self, other) → greater than or equal (>=)

Use Case in Ignition

- Filter out **duplicate sensors** in a list
- Sort device objects by **value**, **status**, or **priority**
- Compare runtime or alarm thresholds between different equipment

Why It's Useful in Ignition

- *Makes your custom classes usable in if statements, sorting, and data filtering*

Ideal for:

- *Comparing tag values*
- *Validating control conditions*
- *Tracking equipment equality or thresholds*

Sample Exercises

Exercise 1: Implement __str__ for Readable Output

Objective:

- Define a string representation for a custom object.

Script:

```
class Device:
def __init__(self, name, status):
self.name = name
self.status = status

def __str__(self):
return "Device '{}' is currently '{}'".format(self.name, self.status)

d = Device("Pump A", "Running")
print d
```

What You Learn: How __str__() customizes how objects are printed or logged in Ignition.

Exercise 2: Overload __eq__ to Compare Objects

Objective:

- Define equality between objects based on their internal state.

Script:

```
class TagWrapper:
def __init__(self, path):
self.path = path

def __eq__(self, other):
return isinstance(other, TagWrapper) and self.path == other.path

a = TagWrapper("[Site A]Pump/Running")
b = TagWrapper("[Site A]Pump/Running")
c = TagWrapper("[Site A]Valve/Running")

print "a == b:", a == b
print "a == c:", a == c
```

What You Learn: How to use __eq__() for meaningful object comparison.

Exercise 3: Add Two Custom Objects with __add__

Objective:

· Implement a class that supports the + operator.

Script:

```
class Runtime:
def __init__(self, hours):
self.hours = hours

def __add__(self, other):
return Runtime(self.hours + other.hours)

def __str__(self):
return str(self.hours) + " hours"

r1 = Runtime(10)
r2 = Runtime(15)
print "Total runtime:", r1 + r2
```

What You Learn: How __add__() can enable custom addition logic.

Exercise 4: Use __len__ to Represent Collection Size

Objective:

· Let an object return a count when passed to len().

Script:

```
class Batch:
def __init__(self, items):
self.items = items

def __len__(self):
return len(self.items)

b = Batch(["Mix1", "Mix2", "Mix3"])
print "Batch size:", len(b)
```

What You Learn: How to use __len__() to integrate with built-in Python functions.

Exercise 5: Implement __getitem__ to Enable Indexing

Objective:

· Allow objects to be accessed like lists or dictionaries.

Script:

```
class SensorGroup:
def __init__(self, sensors):
self.sensors = sensors

def __getitem__(self, index):
return self.sensors[index]

group = SensorGroup(["Temp", "Pressure", "Level"])
print "Sensor at 1:", group[1]
```

What You Learn: How to make objects subscriptable with __getitem__.

19

Chapter 19: Working with Databases and Datasets

Ignition scripting allows you to interact with external databases and internal data tables through structured data types known as **datasets**. Datasets represent tabular data and are commonly used to store and display query results, tag history, and component data across Vision and Perspective.

In this chapter, you'll learn how to:

- Create and connect to a database table
- Insert, update, and retrieve records using Ignition scripting
- Work with datasets to process and present data
- Use scripting to power data-driven automation logic

By the end, you'll understand how to build efficient, scalable solutions that depend on real-time or historical data stored in your Ignition database.

19.1 Creating the Table and Inserting Initial Records

Before using Ignition to interact with a database, you must ensure that the necessary table structure exists within your database. For this chapter, we'll use a MySQL database connection named **IgnitionMySql**, and a simple table called **test** with two fields: userID and username.

Step 1: Create the Table in MySQL

Run this SQL command using your database management tool:

This creates a basic table where each record has a unique, auto-incrementing ID and a username string.

```
CREATE TABLE test (
    userID INT PRIMARY KEY AUTO_INCREMENT,
    username VARCHAR(100)
);
```

This creates a basic table where each record has a unique, auto-incrementing ID and a username string.

Step 2: Insert a Record Manually (Optional)

You can add a test record manually using:

```
INSERT INTO test (username) VALUES ('admin');
```

Step 3: Insert a Record from Ignition

You can also insert new records programmatically using system.db.runPrep Update() inside a script:

```
system.db.runPrepUpdate(
  "INSERT INTO test (username) VALUES (?)",
  ["operator1"],
  "IgnitionMySql"
)
```

This is a **prepared statement**, which ensures safe handling of user input and prevents SQL injection.

If you want to insert **multiple records** (e.g., operator1, operator2, mainte- nance1) into the test table using a **single script block**, you have two clean options in Ignition scripting:

Option 1: Use a Loop with runPrepUpdate

This is the safest and most readable way:

```
usernames = ["operator1", "operator2", "maintenance1"]

for name in usernames:
  system.db.runPrepUpdate(
    "INSERT INTO test (username) VALUES (?)",
    [name],
    "IgnitionMySql"
  )
```

· Executes one insert per user
· Uses prepared statements for security

- Easy to manage or modify later

Option 2: Use a Single SQL Statement (Not Recommended for Dynamic Input)

You can technically build a multi-row insert, but **it's not parameterized**, so it should only be used with **hardcoded, trusted values**:

```
query = """
INSERT INTO test (username) VALUES
('operator1'), ('operator2'), ('maintenance1')
"""

system.db.runUpdateQuery(query, "IgnitionMySql")
```

- **Faster**, but lacks security if user input is involved
- Not compatible with runPrepUpdate()
- Good only for static or initial setup

Best Practice for Ignition

Stick with **Option 1** (loop with runPrepUpdate) for clarity, maintainability, and security — especially in production systems or when usernames are dynamically generated.

19.2 Converting Datasets to PyDatasets for Python Scripting

When you query a database or access a component's data in Ignition, the result is returned as a **Dataset** — a powerful, but non-iterable table structure specific to Ignition. However, in Jython scripts, you'll often need to work with this data using Python-style loops and indexing.

To do that, you must first convert the Dataset to a **PyDataSet** using:

```
pyData = system.dataset.toPyDataSet(results)
```

This conversion wraps the original Dataset, allowing you to use standard Python idioms like for row in ..., list-style indexing, and direct access to column names.

Example: Iterating Over a Query Result

```
results = system.db.runQuery("SELECT userID, username FROM test",
"IgnitionMySql")
pyData = system.dataset.toPyDataSet(results)

for row in pyData:
    print row["userID"], row["username"]
```

This approach is essential when processing query results, building dynamic logic, or passing structured data into components.

Always convert Datasets before iteration when scripting in Jython — especially when working with queries, tag history, table components, or named queries. This ensures your scripts run smoothly and behave like native Python code.

19.3 Reading from and Writing to Databases

Ignition allows you to interact with your database using built-in scripting functions. When reading and writing, always use **prepared statements** with parameter placeholders (?) to ensure security and proper data handling.

Reading User Records from the Database

Assume your test table contains the following users: operator1, operator2, and maintenance1.

Use system.db.runPrepQuery() to select specific user data:

```
query = "SELECT userID, username FROM test WHERE username IN (?, ?, ?)"
data = system.db.runPrepQuery(query, ["operator1", "operator2",
"maintenance1"], "IgnitionMySql")
pyData = system.dataset.toPyDataSet(data)

for row in pyData:
    print "User ID:", row["userID"], "| Username:", row["username"]
```

This safely retrieves and prints all three users from the test table.

Writing New User Records to the Database

To insert users into the database using Ignition scripting:

```
usernames = ["operator1", "operator2", "maintenance1"]

for name in usernames:
    system.db.runPrepUpdate(
        "INSERT INTO test (username) VALUES (?)",
        [name],
        "IgnitionMySql"
    )
```

This loop inserts each user as a new record. If these users already exist, consider adding a uniqueness constraint or using an UPDATE instead.

Ignition Script to Create the logs Table

This script will create a simple logs table with an auto-increment ID, a username, an action, and a timestamp.

```
createQuery = """
CREATE TABLE IF NOT EXISTS logs (
    logID INT PRIMARY KEY AUTO_INCREMENT,
    user VARCHAR(100),
    action VARCHAR(255),
    timestamp DATETIME DEFAULT CURRENT_TIMESTAMP
)
"""

# Run the query using runUpdateQuery()
system.db.runUpdateQuery(createQuery, "IgnitionMySql")
```

Table Fields:

- logID: Unique identifier (auto-incremented)
- user: The user performing the action
- action: Description of what the user did
- timestamp: Automatically filled with the current date and time when a new row is inserted

Logging User Actions

- You can log actions performed by users with a separate table (e.g., logs):

```
query = "INSERT INTO logs (user, action) VALUES (?, ?)"
system.db.runPrepUpdate(query,
            ["operator1",
            "Logged In"
            ],
            "IgnitionMySql"
            )
system.db.runPrepUpdate(query,
            ["operator2",
            "Started Process"
            ],
            "IgnitionMySql"
            )
system.db.runPrepUpdate(query,
            ["maintenance1",
            "Reset Alarm"
            ],
            "IgnitionMySql"
            )
```

Each line adds a new row into the logs table, associating a user with a system action.

Example: Updating a Username in the Database

Suppose your table contains the user maintenance1, and you want to change it to maintenance. Use system.db.runPrepUpdate() with a WHERE clause:

```
# Update username from 'maintenance1' to 'maintenance'
query = "UPDATE test SET username = ? WHERE username = ?"
system.db.runPrepUpdate(query, ["maintenance",
            "maintenance1"
            ],
            "IgnitionMySql"
            )
```

What This Does:

- username = ? sets the new value (maintenance)
- WHERE username = ? finds the original (maintenance1)
- "IgnitionMySql" is the name of the database connection

Confirm the Update

After the update, you can confirm it with a quick query:

```
data = system.db.runPrepQuery("SELECT * FROM test WHERE username = ?",
["maintenance"], "IgnitionMySql")
pyData = system.dataset.toPyDataSet(data)

for row in pyData:
    print "Updated User:", row["username"]
```

This ensures your script updated the record successfully.

19.4 Use Scripting to Power Data-Driven Automation Logic

Ignition scripting allows you to make real-time decisions and drive UI or control logic based on database data. To enable this, always convert query results into a **PyDataSet**, which gives you full access to loop through rows, apply conditions, and trigger actions.

```
# Run a database query
results = system.db.runQuery("SELECT userid, username FROM test",
"IgnitionMySql")

# Convert Dataset to PyDataSet for Python-style iteration
pyData = system.dataset.toPyDataSet(results)

# Use logic to react to data
for row in pyData:
  username = row["username"]
  if username == "operator1":
    print "Send alert to:", username
    # Insert automation logic here, e.g., system.tag.write(), send email, set a
property, etc.
  elif username == "maintenance1":
    print "Flag for maintenance access"
  else:
    print "User recognized:", username
```

results = system.db.runQuery("SELECT userid, username FROM test", "IgnitionMySql")

- This line **executes a SQL query** against the database named "Ignition-MySql".
- It selects two columns, userid and username, from the table test.
- The result is returned as a Dataset, which isn't directly iterable like a list.

pyData = system.dataset.toPyDataSet(results)

- Since Dataset objects don't behave like normal Python lists, we convert it to a **PyDataSet**.
- PyDataSet allows you to **loop through rows easily** and **access columns by name**, like a dictionary.

for row in pyData:

- **Start a loop** through each row of the PyDataSet.
- row is a **dictionary-like object** where you can access columns by their names.

username = row["username"]

- Pull the value from the username column in the current row.
- Store it in a Python variable called username for easy use.

if username == "operator1":

print "Send alert to:", username

- If the username is "operator1", it **prints** a message saying to send an alert.
- (Comment suggests you could trigger real automation here — like writing to a tag or sending an email.)

elif username == "maintenance1":

print "Flag for maintenance access"

- If the username is "maintenance1", it **prints** a different message, suggesting special handling for maintenance.

else:

print "User recognized:", username

- For **all other users** not named "operator1" or "maintenance1", it just acknowledges the user.

Practical Use Cases:

- **Trigger Tag Writes** based on user roles or active tasks.
- **Show/Hide UI Elements** depending on user status or access level.
- **Send Email or Notification** when certain users or conditions are detected.
- **Auto-Populate Dropdowns or Power Tables** dynamically with filtered data.

Sample Exercises

Exercise 1: Create and Populate a Table

Objective:

- Create a new table and insert multiple records into it.

Script:

```
system.db.runUpdateQuery("""
CREATE TABLE users (
  userId INT PRIMARY KEY AUTO_INCREMENT,
  username VARCHAR(50)
);
""", "IgnitionMySql")

system.db.runUpdateQuery("""
INSERT INTO users (username) VALUES
('operator1'),
('operator2'),
('maintenance1');
""", "IgnitionMySql")
```

What You Learn: How to create a table and insert initial records into a database using Ignition scripting.

Exercise 2: Convert a Dataset to a PyDataSet

Objective:

· Fetch data from a table and convert it for easy Python-style looping.

Script:

```
results = system.db.runQuery("SELECT * FROM users", "IgnitionMySql")
pyData = system.dataset.toPyDataSet(results)

for row in pyData:
    print "Username:", row["username"]
```

What You Learn: How to retrieve query results and convert them to a PyDataSet for iteration and data manipulation.

Exercise 3: Read and Write to a Database

Objective:

· Read existing records and insert a new record into the same table.

Script:

```
# Read existing users
users = system.db.runQuery("SELECT username FROM users", "IgnitionMySql")
for user in system.dataset.toPyDataSet(users):
    print "Current User:", user["username"]

# Write a new user
system.db.runUpdateQuery("""
INSERT INTO users (username) VALUES ('supervisor1');
""", "IgnitionMySql")
```

What You Learn: How to read from and insert into a database table in Ignition scripting.

Exercise 4: Use Scripting for Decision-Based Automation

Objective:

· Trigger actions based on database values.

Script:

```
users = system.db.runQuery("SELECT username FROM users", "IgnitionMySql")
pyData = system.dataset.toPyDataSet(users)

for row in pyData:
    if row["username"] == "operator1":
        print "Send notification to Operator 1"
    elif row["username"] == "maintenance1":
        print "Flag Maintenance User"
    else:
        print "General User:", row["username"]
```

What You Learn: How to apply conditional automation logic based on live database data.

Exercise 5: Update a Record Based on Logic

Objective:

- Modify a user's information conditionally from a script.

Script:

```
users = system.db.runQuery("SELECT userId, username FROM users",
"IgnitionMySql")
pyData = system.dataset.toPyDataSet(users)

for row in pyData:
  if row["username"] == "operator2":
    system.db.runPrepUpdate(
      "UPDATE users SET username = ? WHERE userId = ?",
      ["operator_backup", row["userId"]],
      "IgnitionMySql"
    )
    print "Updated operator2 to operator_backup"
```

What You Learn: How to dynamically update database records inside a script using real-time data decisions.

20

Chapter 20: Jython and Java Integration Basics

Jython and Java integration in Ignition allows you to access and use Java classes directly within your Python scripts. Since Jython runs on the Java Virtual Machine (JVM), you can import Java libraries using the import statement and interact with Java objects just like native Python ones. This capability is useful for extending functionality, leveraging existing Java tools, or interacting with Ignition's internal APIs. Understanding this integration expands your scripting power by combining Python's simplicity with Java's robust features in Ignition.

20.1 Accessing Java Classes in Jython (Ignition Script Console Edition)

One of the biggest advantages of scripting in Ignition is that you can directly access **Java classes** from your Jython scripts.

This becomes especially useful in the **Ignition Script Console**, where you're often testing ideas, formatting data, or building logic before moving it into a Vision or Perspective component.

Why Use Java Classes in the Script Console?

- To **format data** in ways that system.date can't.
- To explore **real-time date/time**, math, or utility classes.
- To gain **fine control** over how information is displayed or processed.
- To learn how Java and Python work together — a key skill in Ignition development.

Example: Custom Date Formatting with Java

Try this in your Script Console:

```
from java.util import Date
from java.text import SimpleDateFormat

now = Date()
formatter = SimpleDateFormat("EEEE, MMMM d, yyyy HH:mm:ss")
print formatter.format(now)
```

What it does:

- Gets the current date and time.
- Formats it to something like: Friday, April 25, 2025 14:45:12
- You can use any Java date format pattern here — not just the limited options from system.date.

Java Classes You Can Try in the Console

Here are a few useful classes to explore right in the Script Console:

```
from java.lang import Math
print "Square root of 144:", Math.sqrt(144)
print "Value of PI:", Math.PI
```

from java.lang import Math

- This line **imports** Java's built-in Math class.
- java.lang is a standard Java package that contains fundamental classes like Math, String, and Integer.
- By importing Math, you can now use Java's powerful math functions directly inside your Python-style script in Ignition.

print "Square root of 144:", Math.sqrt(144)

- Math.sqrt(144) calls the **square root** function from Java's Math class.
- sqrt stands for "square root."
- It calculates $\sqrt{144}$, which is 12.0.
- The print command displays the result:
- → Square root of 144: 12.0

print "Value of PI:", Math.PI

- Math.PI is a **constant** provided by Java's Math class.
- It holds the value of π (pi), approximately 3.141592653589793.
- The print command displays it:
- → Value of PI: 3.141592653589793

```
from java.util import ArrayList
list = ArrayList()
list.add("Motor")
list.add("Valve")
print list
```

from java.util import ArrayList

- This line **imports** the ArrayList class from Java's standard java.util package.
- ArrayList is like a **dynamic list** — it automatically grows as you add new items.
- You use it when you want to **collect multiple items** and **change the size of the list** easily (just like a Python list, but Java's version).

list = ArrayList()

- This creates a new **empty** ArrayList object named list.
- Right now, it's an empty container ready to store industrial system components.

list.add("Motor")

list.add("Valve")

- list.add("Motor") adds the word "Motor" to the list.
- list.add("Valve") adds the word "Valve" to the list.
- You are **building a dynamic collection** of device types — imagine this as **a list of critical plant equipment** that you're tracking.

print list

- This prints out the contents of the list.

Output would look like:

```
[Motor, Valve]
```

In a real automation project, you could use ArrayList to:

- Build a list of devices that need inspection.
- Track components that triggered alarms.
- Collect all equipment running in "manual mode" for review.

20.2 Using Java Packages with import

In Ignition, you can also import **entire Java packages** — not just individual classes — to perform very specific tasks that are especially helpful in industrial HMI and SCADA projects.

One common package is java.lang, which gives you access to system-level information like the current time, operating system, and user details.

Practical Examples for HMI Development

```
from java.lang import System
print "Timestamp (ms):", System.currentTimeMillis()
```

Useful for recording when an operator presses a button or when a device state changes.

Check System Environment Info

```
from java.lang import System
print "Operating System:", System.getProperty("os.name")
print "Username:", System.getProperty("user.name")
```

Useful for identifying which client or machine is connected when troubleshooting alarms or sessions.

Format a Unique Event ID

```
from java.lang import System
event_id = "EVENT_" + str(System.currentTimeMillis())
print "Generated Event ID:", event_id
```

Quickly generate a unique event or alarm ID based on the exact timestamp.

- *When you need low-level system values — such as timestamps, OS info, user info, or session identifiers —*
- *importing Java packages gives you flexibility beyond what Ignition's*

system.* functions alone provide.

20.3 Creating and Working with Java Objects

In Ignition scripting, you can **create Java objects** and work with them just like you would with Python objects.

When you import a Java class, you can create an instance (object) by simply calling it with parentheses (), passing in any required parameters.

This is extremely useful when customizing how screens look or behave inside **Vision Clients**, especially when dealing with **colors, fonts, sizes, or graphical elements**.

Example – Creating a Color Object

```
from java.awt import Color

red = Color(255, 0, 0)
print red.getRed()   # Output: 255
print red.getGreen() # Output: 0
print red.getBlue()  # Output: 0
```

- from java.awt import Color imports the Color class from Java's graphics package.
- Color(255, 0, 0) creates a **red color object** by setting RGB (Red, Green, Blue) values.
- .getRed(), .getGreen(), and .getBlue() let you retrieve individual color components.
- In an HMI screen, you could use this color to dynamically set the background of a button, change the color of a label, or highlight alarms.

Use CaseExample

- Change the color of a motor status indicator - Set background to green if motor is running
- Highlight an alarm label - Flash red when an alarm is active
- Customize button colors based on PLC feedback - Show yellow for manual mode, blue for auto mode
- Format table rows in Vision Power Tables - Color code values by thresholds (safe, warning, danger)

More Java Objects Commonly Used in Vision Scripting

Fonts:

```
from java.awt import Font
boldFont = Font("Arial", Font.BOLD, 14)
```

Dimensions (Sizes):

```
from java.awt import Dimension
size = Dimension(100, 50)  # Width 100, Height 50
```

Points (Positions):

```
from java.awt import Point
location = Point(200, 150)  # X=200, Y=150
```

All of these Java objects can be used to **adjust Vision components** dynamically at runtime with scripting.

- *After you create a Java object, you call methods on it using a period (.), just like with Python objects.*
- *Most Java classes have built-in getters and setters like getRed(), getFontName(), or setSize().*
- *Use the Script Console to test creating objects before moving them into button events or client scripts.*

20.4 Calling Java Methods and Using Java Properties

When working with Java objects inside Ignition scripting, you **call methods** exactly the same way you would call a function in Python — using parentheses () after the method name.

This is especially important when interacting with **Vision components**, because many Vision objects are actually Java Swing components under the hood.

Example – Calling a Java Method

```
from java.util import Random

rand = Random()
print rand.nextInt(100)
```

- from java.util import Random imports the Java Random class.
- rand = Random() creates a new random number generator object.
- rand.nextInt(100) calls the nextInt() method, asking for a random integer between 0 and 99.
- The method call behaves **just like a Python function** — parentheses are required.

Accessing Java Properties with Getters and Setters

Java objects often expose internal data using special methods called **getters** and **setters**:

- A **getter** retrieves a value: getSomething()
- A **setter** changes a value: setSomething(value)

Example using a Color object:

```
from java.awt import Color

color = Color(0, 128, 255)
print "Blue component:", color.getBlue()

# No setter for Color since it's immutable, but in many cases you'd use
setX(value)
```

You **call them like normal methods** to retrieve or set properties of Java objects.

Example – Using a Vision Button's Java Methods

In a real Vision window scripting an event like actionPerformed, you could do:

```
from java.awt import Color

# Set button background color to green when clicked
event.source.setBackground(Color(0, 255, 0))

# Get the current text of the button
text = event.source.getText()
print "Button says:", text
```

- *event.source refers to the Vision component (e.g., a Button).*
- *You call setBackground() to change its color.*
- *You call getText() to retrieve its current label.*
- *Always use parentheses () even for simple getters like getText().*
- *When you see something like .background or .font on a Vision component, it's really a Java object — and you can dig deeper using its own getters and setters.*
- *Testing your calls first in the Script Console helps avoid mistakes in live Vision windows.*

20.5 Practical Integration Use in Ignition

When scripting in Ignition, you can import and use Java classes directly. This provides powerful tools beyond basic Python functionality, useful for Vision components, system information, randomization, and more.

Advanced Date Formatting:

- Use java.text.SimpleDateFormat to create precise timestamps for logs or dynamic file names.

Example:

```
from java.text import SimpleDateFormat
from java.util import Date

sdf = SimpleDateFormat("yyyy-MM-dd_HH-mm-ss")
now = Date()
formattedDate = sdf.format(now)
print formattedDate
```

Random Numbers:

- Use java.util.Random for generating random integers or floats, perfect for test data or mockups.

Example:

```
from java.util import Random

rand = Random()
randomNumber = rand.nextInt(100)  # Random integer between 0-99
print randomNumber
```

System Info:

- Access java.lang.System to retrieve system properties like operating system, memory usage, or Java version.

Example:

```
from java.lang import System

osName = System.getProperty("os.name")
javaVersion = System.getProperty("java.version")
print "OS:", osName
print "Java Version:", javaVersion
```

Vision Component Styling:

- Use Java's AWT classes such as java.awt.Color to directly modify Vision component properties.

Example:

```
from java.awt import Color

event.source.background = Color(0, 128, 255)  # Set background to blue
```

String Handling:

- Leverage java.lang.String for advanced string manipulation—splitting, matching, regex—although native Python methods are often simpler.

Example:

```
from java.lang import String

JString = String("Hello, World")
parts = JString.split(", ")
print parts[0]  # Output: Hello
print parts[1]  # Output: World
```

Sample Exercises

Exercise 1: Import and Use a Java Class

- **Objective**: Use the java.util.Date class to get and print the current time.

Script:

```
from java.util import Date

now = Date()
print "Current Java date and time:", now
```

What You Learn: How to import and use a basic Java class in Jython.

Exercise 2: Use java.text.SimpleDateFormat for Custom Formatting

· **Objective**: Format a Java date object using Java–style formatting.

Script:

```
from java.util import Date
from java.text import SimpleDateFormat

formatter = SimpleDateFormat("yyyy-MM-dd HH:mm:ss")
now = Date()
formatted = formatter.format(now)
print "Formatted date:", formatted
```

What You Learn: How to format dates using Java's powerful formatting tools.

Exercise 3: Use a Java ArrayList

· **Objective**: Use java.util.ArrayList to build a dynamic list in Java style.

Script:

```
from java.util import ArrayList

devices = ArrayList()
devices.add("Pump1")
devices.add("Pump2")
devices.add("Valve1")

for d in devices:
    print d
```

What You Learn: How to use Java collections alongside native Python types.

Exercise 4: Call Java Methods on a Java Object

- **Objective**: Use Java methods and properties from within Jython.

Script:

```
from java.lang import String

s = String("Ignition")
print "Uppercase:", s.toUpperCase()
print "Length:", s.length()
```

What You Learn: How to access Java methods and properties like .toUpperCase() and .length() in Jython.

Exercise 5: Combine Ignition and Java – Logging with java.util.logging.Logger

- **Objective**: Use Java's native logging mechanism (in addition to Ignition's logger).

Script:

```
ffrom java.util.logging import Logger

log = Logger.getLogger("JavaLogger")
log.info("Hello from Java's built-in logger!")
```

What You Learn: How to tap into Java-based libraries for advanced system control and output.

21

Chapter 21: Working with Java Swing

Working with Java Swing in Ignition Vision allows you to access and customize GUI components beyond the standard scripting interface. Using Jython, you can import Swing classes to manipulate elements like buttons, labels, or tables directly, enabling advanced UI behaviors or styling. This is especially useful in Vision clients for dynamic component control or integrating custom dialogs. Understanding Java Swing access gives Ignition Vision developers deeper control over client interfaces and expands the creative possibilities of Vision scripting.

21.1 Overview of Java Swing in Vision Clients

Ignition Vision is built on top of **Java Swing**, a mature Java-based GUI framework. This means that every Vision component — buttons, labels, text fields, tables, etc. — is actually a **Java Swing object** under the hood.

As a result, you can go beyond what the Ignition Designer exposes and directly modify the component's appearance, behavior, and layout using Java classes such as java.awt.Color, java.awt.Font, and javax.swing.* through Jython scripts.

Inspecting the Java Class Type of a Component

When using event.source, you get a direct reference to the component that triggered the event. You can then use Python's type() function to see what Swing class backs it.

```
from javax.swing import JOptionPane

button = event.source
button_type = type(button)

# Get a logger instance
logger = system.util.getLogger("SwingDebug")

# Log the button type
logger.info("This component is a: {}".format(button_type))
```

This tells you you're working with a javax.swing.JButton object — and can therefore use Java methods and properties from that class.

from javax.swing import JOptionPane

This line imports the **JOptionPane** class from Java Swing, which is used to create dialog boxes. While it's not used later in this snippet, it's included if you also want to show a popup message. You can remove this line if you're not using dialogs.

button = event.source

event.source refers to the component that triggered the event — in this case, a button. This line assigns that component to the variable button.

button_type = type(button)

This gets the **Java class type** of the component (e.g., <type 'javax.swing.JBut ton'>) and stores it in the variable button_type.

logger = system.util.getLogger("SwingDebug")

This creates or retrieves a **named logger** called "SwingDebug". This logger will send messages to the **Output Console** in the Designer and the **Logs** section in the Gateway (Diagnostics).

logger.info("This component is a: {}".format(button_type))

This sends an **info-level log message** that includes the Java class type of the component.

This script is useful for debugging and teaching — it shows how Vision components are Java Swing objects and helps confirm exactly what kind of Swing class you're working with.

21.2 Creating Simple Swing Windows (Designer-Only Use)

In Ignition Vision, you can directly create and display **Java Swing windows** using Jython, thanks to its ability to access Java classes. This is useful for **prototyping custom interfaces**, showing developer-only debug windows, or exploring how Swing works. However, this technique is **not recommended for production** Vision applications and should **never be used in Gateway scripts** or Perspective.

```
from javax.swing import JFrame, JLabel

# Create a new JFrame (window)
frame = JFrame("Test Window")

# Create a label and add it to the frame
label = JLabel("Hello, Ignition + Swing!")
frame.add(label)

# Set window size and make it visible
frame.setSize(300, 100)
frame.setVisible(True)
```

from javax.swing import JFrame, JLabel

This line **imports two Java Swing classes**:

- JFrame: A standard top-level window (like a regular desktop app window).
- JLabel: A simple GUI component that displays a line of text or an image.

frame = JFrame("Test Window")

This creates a new instance of JFrame with the title "Test Window" shown in the title bar.

- This window exists **outside** of the Ignition Vision window system — it's a native Java window.

label = JLabel("Hello, Ignition + Swing!")

This creates a label that will display the text "Hello, Ignition + Swing!".

- Labels are typically used to show static text in a GUI.

frame.add(label)

This adds the label to the frame.

- By default, Swing uses a basic layout manager that will center the label in the window.

frame.setSize(300, 100)

This sets the size of the window to **300 pixels wide** and **100 pixels tall**.

- If you don't set a size, the window may not appear or may be too small to see.

frame.setVisible(True)

This makes the window visible.

- Without this, the frame is created but remains hidden.

This script creates a simple, standalone Java Swing window with a label inside. It's great for prototyping or exploring Swing features within Ignition, but it runs outside the normal Ignition Vision windowing system, so it's not suitable for production use.

21.3 Enhancing Vision Tooltips with Swing

While Ignition Vision allows basic tooltips through the tooltipText property, Java Swing gives you **advanced control** over how tooltips behave and appear. This includes customizing **delay times**, **popup durations**, and even **HTML-styled content** using ToolTipManager and JComponent methods.

Example: Customize Tooltip Delay and Styling

```
from javax.swing import ToolTipManager
from java.awt import Font

# Get the component that triggered the event
component = event.source

# Set an HTML-styled tooltip
component.setToolTipText("<html><b><font color='blue'>Custom
Tooltip</font></b><br>More info here</html>")

# Customize tooltip display behavior
tipManager = ToolTipManager.sharedInstance()
tipManager.setInitialDelay(100)    # Delay before tooltip shows (ms)
tipManager.setDismissDelay(5000)   # How long tooltip stays visible (ms)
tipManager.setReshowDelay(50)      # Time before reappearing if user
moves away and returns

# Optional: make tooltip font larger
component.setFont(Font("SansSerif", Font.PLAIN, 14))
```

What This Does:

- Adds a **multi-line, HTML-enhanced tooltip** with custom color and formatting.
- Adjusts **how fast the tooltip appears, how long it stays,** and how quickly it can **reappear**.
- Improves usability when explaining complex controls or showing context-sensitive hints.

Real-World Use Cases:

- Guide users in Vision forms with longer, styled tooltips (without building modal help popups).
- Add delay-based tooltips for buttons with destructive actions ("Clicking this will delete...").
- Use as part of an onboarding UX where tooltips act as lightweight helpers.

21.4 Handling Events with Java Listeners

Ignition Vision provides built-in event scripting (like actionPerformed, mousePressed, etc.), which is sufficient for nearly all use cases. However, if you need **custom or multiple event listeners,** or want to tap directly into **Java's event model**, you can attach Java Swing listeners using Jython.

This lets you define reusable or dynamic event handlers programmatically — useful in advanced UIs or dynamic component generation.

```
from java.awt.event import ActionListener

# Define a custom listener class
class MyListener(ActionListener):
  def actionPerformed(self, e):
    system.gui.messageBox("Action triggered!")

# Attach the listener to the button component
event.source.addActionListener(MyListener())
```

What This Does:

- Creates a class MyListener that implements Java's ActionListener interface.
- Defines an actionPerformed method, which runs when the button is clicked.
- Dynamically attaches this listener to the component via .addActionListener(...).

This works because Ignition Vision components are Java Swing objects, such as JButton, which support standard Swing listeners.

Important Notes:

- Java listeners persist **only for the session** — they don't show in Designer after save/load.
- Ignition doesn't expose listener management (e.g., removeActionListener()), so avoid duplicates or reassigning in loops.
- Use this only when **you need multiple handlers**, **reusable logic**, or **advanced interaction** (like global keyboard listeners, dynamic validation, etc.).

21.5 Swing Enhancements in Ignition

Ignition Vision components are Java Swing objects, which means you can access a wide range of Java Swing features not directly exposed in the Designer. This allows you to **dynamically style**, **resize**, or **fine-tune** components at runtime beyond the default property editor or bindings.

These enhancements are perfect for:

- Visual feedback (e.g. warning colors, emphasis).
- User-driven resizing or formatting.
- Runtime customization during scripting events.

Example 1: Change Background Color

MouseEntered script

```
from java.awt import Color

# Set background to yellow
event.source.background = Color(255, 255, 0)
```

from java.awt import Color

This imports the Color class from Java's java.awt package, which is used to define colors in RGB (Red, Green, Blue) format. This class allows you to specify precise color values, like pure red Color(255, 0, 0) or pure yellow Color(255, 255, 0).

event.source.background = Color(255, 255, 0)

This line accesses the component that triggered the script (such as a button or label) via event.source, and then sets its background property to a new Color object with the RGB value **(255, 255, 0)** — which is bright **yellow**.

MouseExited script

```
from java.awt import Color

# Set background to yellow
event.source.background = Color(250, 250, 251)
```

Example 2: Set Font on Labels, Buttons, Inputs

MouseEntered script

```
from java.awt import Font

# Get a reference to the label component by name
label = event.source.parent.getComponent("StyledLabel")

# Change font to Verdana, Italic, size 18
label.font = Font("Verdana", Font.ITALIC, 18)
```

from java.awt import Font

This imports the Font class from Java's java.awt package. The Font class lets you specify the **font family**, **style** (like plain, bold, italic), and **size** for components that display text.

label = event.source.parent.getComponent("StyledLabel")

This line finds the **label named "StyledLabel"** in the same container (like the same Vision window or panel) as the component that triggered the event (usually a button).

- event.source refers to the button that was clicked.
- .parent accesses the container that holds both the button and the label.
- .getComponent("StyledLabel") retrieves the label by its **component name** set in the Property Editor.

MouseExited script

```
from java.awt import Font

# Get a reference to the label component by name
label = event.source.parent.getComponent("StyledLabel")

# Return font to original
label.font = Font("Dialog", Font.PLAIN, 14)
```

Swing access gives you fine-tuned control over Vision UI design when standard bindings aren't enough.

Sample Exercises

Exercise 1: Access the Underlying Java Swing Object

- **Objective**: Retrieve the underlying Java Swing component from a Vision component.

Script (Vision Button → actionPerformed):

```
button = event.source
swingObject = button.getComponent(0)
print "Swing object class:", swingObject.__class__
```

What You Learn: Every Vision component wraps a Java Swing component that can be accessed and manipulated.

Exercise 2: Change Font or Color Using Java Swing

- **Objective**: Modify the font and background color of a label using Java Swing methods.

Script:

```
from java.awt import Font, Color

label = event.source.parent.getComponent("Label")
label.setFont(Font("Arial", Font.BOLD, 18))
label.setBackground(Color.YELLOW)
label.setOpaque(True)
```

What You Learn: How to apply advanced styling with Java AWT/Swing on Vision components.

Exercise 3: Use javax.swing.JOptionPane for a Custom Dialog

- **Objective**: Use a native Swing dialog box instead of system.gui.message Box().

Script:

```
from javax.swing import JOptionPane

JOptionPane.showMessageDialog(None, "Custom Swing Alert Box",
"Notice", JOptionPane.INFORMATION_MESSAGE)
```

What You Learn: How to use native Swing dialog components for notifications or prompts.

Exercise 4: Add a Java Mouse Listener to a Vision Component

- **Objective**: Add a mouse event handler using Swing's MouseAdapter.

Script:

```
from java.awt.event import MouseAdapter

class ClickListener(MouseAdapter):
def mouseClicked(self, e):
print "Swing click detected at:", e.getX(), e.getY()

comp = event.source.parent.getComponent("Label")
comp.addMouseListener(ClickListener())
```

What You Learn: How to enhance component interactivity with Swing listeners.

Exercise 5: Dynamically Change Tooltip Text

- **Objective**: Update the tooltip of a Vision component using Java methods.

Script:

```
field = event.source.parent.getComponent("TextField")
field.setToolTipText("Enter a value between 0 and 100.")
```

What You Learn: How to manipulate Swing tooltips for user guidance.

22

Chapter 22: Java Collections

Java Collections in Ignition scripting provide access to powerful data structures like ArrayList, HashMap, and HashSet through Jython's integration with Java. These collections offer enhanced performance and flexibility for handling large or complex data sets compared to standard Python types. You can use them for organizing tag paths, storing dynamic datasets, or managing mappings between keys and values. Leveraging Java Collections in Ignition enables more efficient, scalable scripts, especially in data-intensive or structured automation scenarios.

22.1 Using Java Lists and Maps in Jython

While Jython in Ignition supports standard Python data types like list and dict, many **Java Swing components** and **Ignition platform features** expect **Java collections**, especially when interacting with Vision tables, datasets, or 3rd-party Java libraries.

To bridge this gap, you can use Java's built-in ArrayList and HashMap to create and pass compatible structures.

```
from java.util import ArrayList

# Create a Java-style list
javaList = ArrayList()
javaList.add("Pump1")
javaList.add("Pump2")

# Access element by index
print javaList.get(0)  # Output: Pump1
```

from java.util import ArrayList

This imports Java's ArrayList class from the java.util package. ArrayList is a **resizable array-like structure** commonly used in Java — similar in behavior to Python's native list, but required by some Java methods and components that don't accept Python lists.

javaList = ArrayList()

This creates a new **Java ArrayList object** called javaList. Initially, it is empty.

Use Cases:

- **Combo Boxes**: Some components like dropdowns or tree models expect Java List objects.
- **Data Models**: Java methods in the Swing API or 3rd-party libraries require ArrayList or HashMap instead of Python-native types.
- **Interfacing with Tag History or Report scripting**, where strict Java typing matters.

javaList.add("Pump1")

javaList.add("Pump2")

These two lines **add elements** to the list using the .add() method (standard for Java lists).

- "Pump1" is added at index 0.
- "Pump2" is added at index 1.

print javaList.get(0) # Output: Pump1

This retrieves the **first element** in the list using .get(0) and prints it.

- In Java ArrayList, elements are accessed using .get(index) instead of square brackets like Python (list[0]).

Summary:

This code demonstrates how to:

- *Import and create a Java-compatible list.*
- *Add elements using .add().*
- *Retrieve values using .get(index).*

It's especially useful when working in Ignition with components (like drop-downs, tables, or Java libraries) that require Java collection types rather than Python-native ones.

22.2 Interoperability Between Python and Java Collections

In Ignition scripting, you often work with both **Python-native** data types (like list, dict) and **Java collections** (ArrayList, HashMap). While Python types work well in most scripts, some Ignition components — especially Vision dropdowns, tables, and external Java APIs — **require Java collections**.

Fortunately, **converting between Python and Java collections is simple**, letting you switch back and forth as needed for compatibility.

Example 1: Convert Python list to Java ArrayList

```
from java.util import ArrayList

pyList = ["A", "B", "C"]
javaList = ArrayList(pyList)
```

- This takes a standard Python list (["A", "B", "C"]) and creates a Java-compatible ArrayList using the constructor.
- This is useful when passing values to components or APIs that require a Java List.

Example 2: Convert Java ArrayList to Python list

```
pyList = list(javaList)
```

- This converts a Java ArrayList (like the one above) back to a standard Python list using Python's built-in list() function.
- This is useful when you want to **loop through or manipulate** Java list data using Python syntax (e.g., slicing, appending).

Use Cases in Ignition:

- Populating Vision **Dropdown Lists**: often expect a java.util.List as a data source.
- Working with **datasets** or **custom Java libraries**: may return Java collections that you'll want to convert to Python for processing.
- Returning **Python lists** to tag event scripts or scripting functions from Java-based logic.

Summary:

- *Use ArrayList(pyList) to convert Python → Java.*
- *Use list(javaList) to convert Java → Python.*
- *This lets you mix Java component compatibility with Python flexibility.*

22.3 Iterating Through Java Collections in Jython

Although Java collections like HashMap and ArrayList aren't native Python types, **Jython allows you to iterate through them using standard Python for loops**. This makes it easy to integrate Java data structures into your scripting logic — especially when interacting with components, datasets, or custom Java APIs inside Ignition.

Example: Iterate Over a Java HashMap

```
from java.util import HashMap

devices = HashMap()
devices.put("Motor1", "Running")
devices.put("Motor2", "Stopped")

for key in devices.keySet():
    print key + " = " + devices.get(key)
```

Line-by-Line Explanation:

from java.util import HashMap

- Imports Java's HashMap class, which is similar to a Python dict.

devices = HashMap()

devices.put("Motor1", "Running")

devices.put("Motor2", "Stopped")

- Iterates over all keys in the HashMap using keySet(). For each key, it prints both the key and its corresponding value. The output would look like:
- **Motor1 = Running**
- **Motor2 = Stopped**

Use Cases in Ignition:

- **Tag event scripts**: Summarize equipment or sensor states.
- **Vision screens**: Dynamically build or update dropdowns or lists based on HashMap values.
- **Gateway scripts**: Process device state maps returned from external systems or libraries.

Summary:

You can use for ... in loops with Java collections like HashMap.keySet() or ArrayList in Jython, making Java object handling feel familiar to Python users.

22.4 Common Java Collection Methods and Patterns

Java's ArrayList and HashMap offer a rich set of methods that are fully usable in Ignition's Jython environment. These methods become especially useful when you're building dynamic UIs, transforming data, or interacting with APIs that return or expect Java collections.

Common ArrayList Methods

```
from java.util import ArrayList

myList = ArrayList()
myList.add("Item1")        # Add an item
myList.add("Item2")
print myList.get(0)        # Access by index → "Item1"
print myList.size()        # Returns number of items → 2
myList.remove("Item1")     # Removes by value
```

Use Cases:

- Populating Vision dropdowns.
- Dynamically storing or updating user input.
- Creating temporary, ordered lists of results.

Common HashMap Methods

```
from java.util import HashMap

myMap = HashMap()
myMap.put("User1", "Active")      # Add key-value pair
myMap.put("User2", "Inactive")
print myMap.get("User1")          # Returns "Active"
print myMap.containsKey("User2")  # Returns True
print myMap.keySet()              # Set of keys → ["User1", "User2"]
print myMap.values()              # Collection of values → ["Active", "Inactive"]
```

Use Cases:

- Tracking the state of devices or users.
- Passing structured parameters to scripting functions.
- Preparing data for display or export in UI components.

Summary of Common Java Collection Methods

ArrayList Methods:

- .add(item) — Adds an item to the end of the list.
- .get(index) — Retrieves the item at the specified position.
- .size() — Returns the number of items in the list.

- .remove(item) — Removes the specified item by value.

HashMap Methods:

- .put(key, value) — Adds or updates a key-value pair.
- .get(key) — Retrieves the value associated with the key.
- .containsKey(key) — Checks if the map contains the specified key.
- .keySet() — Returns a set of all keys.
- .values() — Returns a collection of all values.

22.5 When to Use Java vs Python Collections in Ignition

Choosing between Python and Java collections in Ignition depends on your **use case** and the **component or script context**. Here's when to use each type:

Use Python list / dict when:

- You want fast, simple scripting logic.
- You're processing data internally without passing it to UI components.

Use Java ArrayList / HashMap when:

- You are passing data into Vision components like dropdowns or tables.
- You're interacting with Java-based libraries or APIs that require Java collections.

Use either type when:

- You are building custom datasets or working with dynamic structures.
- You're willing to convert as needed for compatibility.

Example: Populate a Dropdown Using Java ArrayList

```
from java.util import ArrayList

dropdown = event.source
items = ArrayList()
items.add("Start")
items.add("Stop")
dropdown.data = items
```

- This example shows how to create a Java ArrayList and assign it to a dropdown's data property — a common scenario where Java collections are required.

Sample Exercises

Exercise 1: Use a java.util.ArrayList for Dynamic Lists

- **Objective**: Create and populate a Java ArrayList, then iterate through it.

Script:

```
from java.util import ArrayList

devices = ArrayList()
devices.add("Pump1")
devices.add("Pump2")
devices.add("Valve1")

for device in devices:
print "Device:", device
```

What You Learn: How to use ArrayList as a flexible, typed alternative to Python lists.

Exercise 2: Use a HashMap for Key-Value Mapping

- **Objective**: Create a Java HashMap to store tag name/value pairs.

Script:

```
from java.util import HashMap

tagMap = HashMap()
tagMap.put("Temp", 72.5)
tagMap.put("Pressure", 125)
tagMap.put("Level", 89.1)

for key in tagMap.keySet():
print key + ":", tagMap.get(key)
```

What You Learn: How to create and loop through a Java map structure in Jython.

Exercise 3: Store Unique Items with HashSet

- **Objective**: Automatically remove duplicate values using a HashSet.

Script:

```
from java.util import HashSet

alarms = HashSet()
alarms.add("High Temp")
alarms.add("Low Flow")
alarms.add("High Temp") # Duplicate

for alarm in alarms:
print "Active alarm:", alarm
```

What You Learn: How HashSet ensures uniqueness in Java collections.

Exercise 4: Use a LinkedList for Queue-like Behavior

- **Objective**: Create a FIFO list of recent system events.

Script:

```
from java.util import LinkedList

eventQueue = LinkedList()
eventQueue.add("Start system")
eventQueue.add("Check valves")
eventQueue.add("Monitor sensors")

while not eventQueue.isEmpty():
print "Handling:", eventQueue.remove()
```

What You Learn: How LinkedList can function as a queue or stack structure.

Exercise 5: Convert a Python List to a Java ArrayList

· **Objective**: Use a Python list and convert it into a Java collection for Java-based methods.

Script:

```
from java.util import ArrayList

pyList = ["SensorA", "SensorB", "SensorC"]
javaList = ArrayList(pyList)

print "Java list size:", javaList.size()
```

What You Learn: How to initialize a Java collection from Python types for compatibility.

23

Chapter 23: Using Java Libraries

Using Java libraries in Ignition scripting allows you to extend functionality by importing external or built-in Java classes directly into your Jython code. This opens access to powerful tools for tasks like date formatting, encryption, file handling, and more. By leveraging Java's extensive standard library or third-party jars (when configured properly), you can solve complex problems that go beyond core Python capabilities. Integrating Java libraries within Ignition enhances script performance, capability, and interoperability in advanced automation solutions.

23.1 Importing External Java Libraries (JAR Files)

Ignition allows you to **extend its capabilities** by importing external Java libraries packaged as .jar files. This is useful for integrating third-party Java APIs or adding custom functionality that's not available through Ignition's built-in modules.

How to Install a Java Library (JAR)

Place the .jar file in the appropriate directory based on scope:

- For **shared use across all scopes** (Vision, Gateway, Perspective):
- lib/core/common/
- For **Gateway scripts only**:
- lib/core/gateway/
- For **Vision Client scripts only**:
- lib/core/vision/

Restart the **Ignition Gateway** after placing the file.

- This ensures the new library is loaded into Ignition's classpath.

Import the class in your Jython script using standard Java package syntax:

```
from com.example.library import MyJavaClass
```

Important Considerations

- The .jar must be fully **Jython-compatible** — avoid libraries that depend on native code (e.g., C extensions).
- Ensure you understand the **scope** (Gateway vs Vision vs shared).
- Restart is always required for classpath updates to take effect.
- Use Java libraries only when needed — most Ignition features can be handled with built-in scripting.

23.2 Adding to Ignition's Classpath Safely

When extending Ignition with external Java libraries, it's critical to follow best practices to avoid runtime errors, version conflicts, or unexpected behavior.

Guidelines for Safe Integration

Use only pure Java JARs:

- The JAR must not rely on native code (JNI or platform-specific binaries).
- Libraries should be written in 100% Java and be compatible with Jython.

Choose the correct directory based on the target scope:

- lib/core/common/ → Use for libraries shared between Gateway and Vision Clients.
- lib/core/gateway/ → Use for libraries accessed only by Gateway scripts (e.g., tag change scripts, reports, Gateway events).
- lib/core/vision/ → Use for libraries required only in Vision Client scripts.

Avoid version conflicts:

- Don't include JARs that duplicate or clash with existing Ignition platform libraries.
- Be cautious with libraries that use older or newer versions of core Java classes.

Always restart the Ignition Gateway:

- A restart is required any time a JAR is added, removed, or updated.
- Without a restart, the classloader will not pick up the changes.

23.3 Using Common Third-Party Libraries in Ignition

Ignition supports a wide range of third-party Java libraries. These can dramatically expand what you can do in your Jython scripts — from manipulating strings to generating charts or handling encryption.

Recommended Libraries and Their Uses

Apache Commons

- Utilities for strings, numbers, files, and collections
- Great for simplifying repetitive code tasks

JFreeChart

- Advanced chart and graph generation
- Useful for dynamic reporting or custom chart components

Apache POI

- Reading and writing Microsoft Excel files
- Ideal for export/import functionality in Vision or reports

JSON-simple

- Lightweight JSON parsing and generation
- Works well for handling REST responses or WebDev payloads

Bouncy Castle

- Cryptography, hashing, certificate generation
- Helpful for secure communication, digital signatures, or token verification

Example: Using Apache Commons Lang for String Utilities

```
from org.apache.commons.lang3 import StringUtils

print StringUtils.capitalize("Ignition") # Output: Ignition
```

This example capitalizes the first letter of a string using Apache Commons Lang — a very handy utility in text processing scripts.

23.4 Handling Class Conflicts and Errors

When importing third-party Java libraries into Ignition, you may occasionally encounter errors like NoClassDefFoundError or ClassNotFoundException. These usually mean the class loader couldn't locate or initialize a required

Java class.

What to Check First

JAR File Location

- Ensure the .jar is placed in the correct folder (lib/core/common/, gateway/, or vision/) based on your use case.

Gateway Logs

- Open the Gateway web interface and review logs under **Status → Logs** to look for class loading errors or dependency problems.

Bytecode Compatibility

- Avoid libraries compiled for Java 11 or newer unless your Ignition Gateway uses that same Java version.
- Jython may have trouble interpreting classes compiled with —release 11 or higher.

Missing Dependencies

- Check if the library depends on other JARs that must also be included (some libraries require multiple files).

Best Practice

- Always test external libraries in a **development Gateway** before rolling them out to production.
- Avoid hot-reloading JARs in a running system — **restart the Gateway** after any changes to ensure clean classpath loading.
- Keep documentation of all added libraries and versions to simplify future

troubleshooting.

23.5 Best Practices for Java Library Use in Ignition

Using external Java libraries in Ignition can be powerful — but to keep projects clean, stable, and maintainable, follow these best practices:

Best Practices Checklist

Use Java libraries only when necessary

- Rely on built-in Ignition features and Python when possible.

Document each library's purpose

- Keep a record of why it was added and which scripts use it.

Use consistent naming conventions and error handling

- Create wrapper functions to shield the rest of your code from raw Java usage.

Leverage project script modules

- Wrap Java class calls inside Python-style functions for easier use across the project.

Log errors using system.util.getLogger()

- Helps with debugging and visibility when something fails.

Example: Wrapping a Java Class in a Script Module

Create a script module named utilities.stringTools and add:

```
from org.apache.commons.lang3 import StringUtils

def capitalize(text):
    return StringUtils.capitalize(text)
```

Now in any client or Gateway script, you can use:

```
from utilities import stringTools

print stringTools.capitalize("sensor")  # Output: Sensor
```

This approach hides the complexity of Java integration and makes your codebase cleaner, more maintainable, and easier for other developers to understand.

Sample Exercises

Exercise 1: Use java.lang.Math for Advanced Math Operations

- **Objective**: Perform precise mathematical functions using Java's math library.

Script:

```
from java.lang import Math

angle = 45
radians = Math.toRadians(angle)
sinVal = Math.sin(radians)

print "Sin of", angle, "degrees:", sinVal
```

What You Learn: How to access Java math functions for trigonometry, rounding, and constants.

Exercise 2: Generate a UUID with java.util.UUID

· **Objective**: Create unique identifiers using a Java utility class.

Script:

```
from java.util import UUID

id = UUID.randomUUID()
print "Generated UUID:", id
```

What You Learn: How to use Java's UUID class for generating unique keys or IDs.

Exercise 3: Use java.text.SimpleDateFormat for Custom Date Formatting

· **Objective**: Format timestamps for logs and reports.

Script:

```
from java.util import Date
from java.text import SimpleDateFormat

formatter = SimpleDateFormat("yyyy-MM-dd HH:mm:ss")
now = Date()
print "Formatted timestamp:", formatter.format(now)
```

What You Learn: How to format Java Date objects with custom patterns.

Exercise 4: Use java.security.MessageDigest for Hashing

- **Objective**: Create a SHA-256 hash of a string using Java's security library.

Script:

```
from java.security import MessageDigest
from javax.xml.bind import DatatypeConverter

inputString = "IgnitionRocks"
md = MessageDigest.getInstance("SHA-256")
md.update(inputString.encode("utf-8"))
digest = md.digest()
hexHash = DatatypeConverter.printHexBinary(digest)

print "SHA-256:", hexHash
```

What You Learn: How to use Java classes for encryption and message hashing.

Exercise 5: Use a Java Class to Perform Time Zone Conversion

- **Objective**: Convert time across time zones using Java's Calendar and TimeZone.

Script:

```
from java.util import Calendar, TimeZone

calendar = Calendar.getInstance()
calendar.setTimeZone(TimeZone.getTimeZone("UTC"))
utcHour = calendar.get(Calendar.HOUR_OF_DAY)

calendar.setTimeZone(TimeZone.getTimeZone("America/Chicago"))
centralHour = calendar.get(Calendar.HOUR_OF_DAY)

print "UTC hour:", utcHour
print "Central hour:", centralHour
```

What You Learn: How to perform time zone-aware logic with Java's time APIs.

Chapter 24: Scripting in Ignition Perspective

Scripting in Ignition Perspective focuses on writing Python logic to enhance user interactions and dynamically control views in a web-based environment. Unlike Vision, Perspective scripts often use component events, property bindings, and script transforms. You can respond to user input, manipulate component properties, and call tag or database functions using self, value, and system functions. Perspective scripting supports both client-side interactivity and gateway-scope operations, enabling modern, responsive applications within Ignition's mobile-first architecture.

24.1 Understanding the Perspective Scripting Environment

Ignition Perspective offers a powerful, modern web-based visualization system — but its scripting environment works differently than Vision.

Key Differences from Vision

- Perspective uses the **same Jython engine** as Vision.
- Scripts in Perspective **run on the Gateway**, not in the client browser.
- **No system.gui functions** (like message boxes or popup windows).
- Interaction is handled through **bindings**, **messaging**, and **session/page context**.
- Main Script Types in Perspective

Component Event Scripts

- Run in response to user interaction (e.g., onClick, onChange, onAction-Performed).
- Used to update tags, send messages, or trigger other server-side logic.

Message Handlers

- Can be scoped to a view, session, or project.
- Used to pass data and commands between components or scripts across views and sessions.

Bindings with Script Transforms

- Allow dynamic calculation or formatting in response to changes in data or tag values.
- Script transforms run server-side and can return calculated results to components.

Session and Page Event Scripts

- Allow initialization, cleanup, or custom behavior when a user opens a page or starts a session.

Summary

Perspective scripting is context-aware, server-executed, and designed for a stateless, browser-based UI. Learning to use bindings and messaging in place of Vision's client-centric GUI tools is essential for effective Perspective development.

24.2 Accessing and Modifying Component Properties

Perspective scripting doesn't use event.source.getComponent() like Vision. Instead, you interact with components using the **self context object**, which gives you direct access to properties and relationships within a view.

Key Access Methods in Perspective

self

- Refers to the component the script is running on.
- Use it to read or modify its own properties.

self.getSibling("ComponentName")

- Gets a component in the **same container** (e.g., same Flex or Coordinate container).
- Useful for scripts like buttons updating a label next to them.

self.getParent()

- Accesses the **container that holds** the current component.
- Useful when you need to traverse up to reach other siblings or higher-level components.

system.perspective.sendMessage()

- For interacting with **components outside the current container or view**, use messages.

Example: onClick Script That Updates a Label

```
self.getSibling("Label").props.text = "Button clicked!"
```

- This script goes on a **button's onClick event**.
- It finds the sibling component named **"Label"** and sets its props.text property.

Best Practices

- *Always name components clearly in the Designer so you can reference them easily in scripts.*

- *Use self.getSibling() for local changes.*
- *Use messages when updating components across containers, popups, or views.*

24.3 Using Script Transforms in Property Bindings

In Perspective, **script transforms** let you process or reformat the output of a binding using Python. This keeps your UI **dynamic, readable**, and **maintainable** — without needing separate event scripts.

What Is a Script Transform?

- A **transform** is an inline Python function that runs **after the binding evaluates**.
- It lets you take the result of a binding and adjust, format, or substitute it before it's applied to the component.
- You write transforms directly in the **binding editor** under the "Script" transform option.

Example: Uppercase Input with Fallback

```
return value.upper() If value else "UNKNOWN"
```

- This takes a user-entered name or string and converts it to uppercase.
- If no value is entered (i.e., None or empty), it returns "UNKNOWN" as a default.

Ideal Use Cases for Script Transforms

Formatting strings

- Capitalize, truncate, or format names, codes, or labels.

Mapping states to colors

- Return "green" if status is "Running", or "red" if "Faulted".

Creating fallback values

- Return "N/A" if the value is missing or invalid.

Controlling visibility or style

- Return True or False to show/hide a component based on user roles or data.

Best Practice

Use script transforms whenever you're:

- *Modifying how a value is presented, not how it's stored.*
- *Reducing the need for event-driven code or tag change scripts.*
- *Keeping UI logic compact and visually traceable in the binding tree.*

Would you like a state-to-color transform example for status indicators?

24.4 Perspective Messaging: sendMessage and receiveMessage

Perspective's built-in messaging system allows components, views, and sessions to **communicate without direct wiring**. This helps you decouple logic and simplify component interactions.

What Messaging Does

- Enables **indirect communication** between components.
- Allows actions in one part of a view to **trigger updates elsewhere**.
- Works across **views, popups, or session-scoped scripts**.

How to Set Up Messaging

Step 1: Add a Message Handler to a Component

- Right-click a component → Add Script → **Message Handler**.
- Give it a name (e.g., updateLabel), then use:

```
def handleMessage(payload):
    self.props.text = payload["message"]
```

Step 2: Send the Message from Another Component

```
system.perspective.sendMessage(
  messageType="updateLabel",
  payload={"message": "Hello!"},
  scope="page"
)
```

Scope Options

- "view" – Messages stay within the same view.
- "page" – Reaches all views on the same tab or page.
- "session" – Sends to every open page/view in the user session.
- "project" – Sends to all sessions in the current project (advanced use).

Real-World Uses

- A **button click** updates a **label or chart** elsewhere on the screen.
- User selections in one view **trigger updates** in another popup.
- A login/logout action sends session-wide **theme or role updates**.

24.5 Session and Page-Level Events

Perspective allows you to run scripts in response to lifecycle events at the **session** and **page** level. These scripts are ideal for initializing data, storing user info, managing state, and performing cleanup actions.

Where to Configure

- Go to the **Perspective section** in the Project Browser.
- Expand **Session Events** or **Page Configuration**.
- Use built-in event hooks like onStartup, onShutdown, and onLogout.

Common Session Event Types

onStartup

- Runs when a new session is opened. Ideal for initializing user-specific settings or variables.

onShutdown

- Runs when a session ends. Useful for cleanup, logging, or releasing locks.

onLogout

- Triggers when a user logs out. Often used for audit tracking or session logging.

onSessionEvent

- Handles data related to the user's session like geolocation, device type, or browser.

Example: Initialize Role on Session Start

```
def onStartup(session):
    session.custom.userRole = session.props.auth.user.roles[0]
```

- This script runs when the session begins.
- It stores the user's primary role into a custom property for easy reference

in views.

Why Use Session and Page Events

- *Centralize logic that would otherwise be repeated across multiple views.*
- *Set default values, language preferences, or access controls based on user identity.*
- *Handle device-specific adjustments (e.g., mobile vs desktop).*
- *Clean up resources or trigger alerts when a user session ends.*

Sample Exercises

Exercise 1: Use onClick to Update a Component Property

- **Objective**: Change the text of a label when a button is clicked.

Steps:

- Add a Button and a Label to the same container.
- Add this script to the Button's onClick event:

```
self.getSibling("Label").props.text = "Button clicked!"
```

What You Learn: How to access and modify sibling components using Perspective scripting.

Exercise 2: Add a Script Transform to a Property Binding

- **Objective**: Format a temperature value to display with a °F symbol.

Steps:

- Bind a Label's props.text to a tag (e.g., [default]Boiler/Temp).
- In the binding, add a **Script Transform**:

```
return str(value) + " °F" if value is not None else "N/A"
```

What You Learn: **How to use script transforms for dynamic formatting in bindings.**

Exercise 3: Send and Receive Messages Between Components

- **Objective**: Use Perspective's messaging system to update one component from another.

Steps:

- On a Button, add this script to onClick:

```
system.perspective.sendMessage(
                    "updateLabel",
                    payload={"msg": "Message received!"},
                    scope="page"
                    )
```

- On a Label component, add a **Message Handler** named updateLabel:

```
def handleMessage(payload):
    self.props.text = payload["msg"]
```

What You Learn: How to use sendMessage() and custom handlers to decouple logic across views.

Exercise 4: Store and Use Session Properties

- **Objective**: Save the selected user role and display it across views.

Steps:

- In a view, run this script (e.g., on a dropdown selection change):

```
self.session.custom.userRole = self.props.value
```

- In another view, bind a Label's text to:

```
session.custom.userRole
```

What You Learn: How to store shared data at the session level for access across views.

Exercise 5: Use system.perspective.navigate() to Switch Views

- **Objective**: Navigate from one view to another on a button click.

Script:

```
system.perspective.navigate("/main/dashboard")
```

What You Learn: How to programmatically navigate between Perspective views.

25

Chapter 25: Scripting Automation Tasks

Scripting automation tasks in Ignition allows you to control processes, manage equipment, and respond to system events using Python. Common tasks include writing to tags, executing sequences, handling timers, and coordinating machine states. Scripts can run in Vision, Perspective, or Gateway scope, using tools like system.tag.writeBlocking(), system.util.in vokeLater(), and control structures to build logic. Automating tasks with scripts improves efficiency, consistency, and responsiveness in industrial applications, enabling customized behavior tailored to operational needs.

25.1 Automating Tag Operations

In Ignition, many tasks involve **reading from** or **writing to multiple tags**. Automating these operations makes scripts cleaner, faster, and more scalable — especially for control actions, status monitoring, or batch updates.

```
tags = ["[Site A]Motors/Motor 1/Speed", "[Site A]Motors/Motor 2/Speed"]
values = system.tag.readBlocking(tags)

for i in range(len(tags)):
    print tags[i], "=", values[i].value
```

- Uses system.tag.readBlocking() to get current values of multiple tags.
- Iterates through results and prints each tag's path and value.
- .value extracts the actual tag value from the returned QualifiedValue.

Writing Multiple Tags

```
paths = ["[Site A]Motors/Motor 1/Start", "[Site A]Motors/Motor 2/Start"]
values = [1, 1]
system.tag.writeBlocking(paths, values)
```

- Uses system.tag.writeBlocking() to write values to multiple tags at once.
- Each item in values corresponds to the matching tag in paths.
- Ensures synchronous writing before the script proceeds.

Common Use Cases

- *Button scripts to control multiple devices at once.*
- *Gateway tag event scripts for handling alarms or state changes.*
- *Scheduled scripts to reset counters or update tag values periodically.*
- *User role-based control to enable or disable equipment groups.*

25.2 Automating Dataset Processing

Datasets are a core part of working with tables, queries, and reports in Ignition. Jython allows you to efficiently **loop through**, **filter**, and **manipulate** these datasets for automation, analysis, or export.

Example: Scanning a Table for Fault Status

```
table = event.source.parent.getComponent("Table")
ds = table.data

for row in range(ds.rowCount):
    value = ds.getValueAt(row, "Status")
    if value == "Fault":
        print "Alert on row", row
```

- Accesses a Vision table component and grabs its .data property (a dataset).
- Loops through each row using range(ds.rowCount).
- Uses getValueAt(row, columnName) to inspect a column named "Status".
- Prints an alert if any row contains the value "Fault".

Common Dataset Automation Tasks

- **Filter rows** based on status, values, or timestamps.
- **Transform data** for formatting, unit conversion, or conditional logic.
- **Summarize data** (e.g., count of alarms, total runtime).
- **Export to CSV** or Excel using scripting or reporting tools.
- **Trigger actions** when conditions are met (e.g., visual alerts or tag writes).

Tip

- Datasets are **immutable**, so to make changes (e.g., highlighting, row removal), use system.dataset.toDataSet() or convert to a PyDataSet for advanced operations.
- Would you like an example that builds a new dataset containing only non-fault rows?

25.3 Scheduling and Delaying Tasks

Ignition provides tools to **schedule**, **delay**, or **repeat** tasks either in the **Vision client** or on the **Gateway**. These tools are essential for time-based automation, background processing, or UI responsiveness.

Delaying Tasks in Vision: system.util.invokeLater()

```
def delayed():
    system.gui.messageBox("This ran after a delay.")

system.util.invokeLater(delayed, 2000)  # 2-second delay
```

- Runs the delayed() function **2 seconds later** (2000 milliseconds).
- Only works in **Vision clients**, not in Perspective or Gateway scripts.
- Useful for deferring UI updates or showing a message after an animation completes.

Running Periodic Scripts in Gateway: Timer Scripts

- Use **Gateway Timer Scripts** for background automation tasks.
- Found in **Project → Gateway Event Scripts → Timer**.
- Set interval (e.g., every 5 seconds, every minute) and script logic.

Common Use Cases

- *Log system health (e.g., CPU load, memory usage).*
- *Synchronize data with external APIs or SQL databases.*
- *Monitor alarms or run logic on production metrics.*
- *Enforce cooldowns or retries in Vision without blocking UI.*

25.4 Creating Reusable Utility Functions

To keep your Ignition projects clean and maintainable, create **reusable script modules** in the **Project Library.** These functions centralize logic, reduce duplication, and make your code easier to troubleshoot and scale.

How to Create a Script Module

- Navigate to **Project > Scripting > Script Library**.
- Create a folder (e.g., utilities) and a script (e.g., control.py).
- Add reusable functions inside:

```
# project.utilities.control.py
def startDevice(deviceTag):
    system.tag.writeBlocking([deviceTag + "/Start"], [1])
```

· This function starts any device by writing 1 to its Start tag.

How to Call It from Anywhere in the Project

```
from project.utilities import control
control.startDevice("[Site A]Motors/Motor 1")
```

· Import the module using its path under the project namespace.
· Call the function just like a normal Python method.

Why Use Script Modules

· *Reduces redundancy across buttons, tag events, or Gateway scripts.*
· *Centralizes business logic, so you only update code in one place.*
· *Improves readability by moving low-level details out of your UI scripts.*
· *Simplifies testing and debugging.*

25.5 Example: Auto-Acknowledge Alarms on Condition

Ignition scripting allows you to programmatically monitor and act on alarm conditions — such as auto-acknowledging specific alarms when business logic is met.

Example: Auto-Acknowledge Alarms for a Specific Device

```
alarms = system.alarm.queryStatus(state=["ActiveUnacked"])
for alarm in alarms.getResults():
  if alarm.get("source").endswith("TestDevice"):
    system.alarm.acknowledge([alarm.get("id")])
```

- Queries all alarms that are **Active and Unacknowledged**.
- Loops through each alarm result.
- Checks if the alarm source ends with "TestDevice".
- Acknowledges the alarm by passing its ID to system.alarm.acknowledge ().

Use Cases

- **Auto-acknowledge test or simulation alarms** to reduce clutter.
- **Reset tags** or perform logic when specific alarms are raised.
- **Trigger alerts** to operators or maintenance based on alarm content.
- **Filter and log alarms** for compliance or reporting purposes.

Best Practice

- *Use caution with auto-acknowledgement — ensure it's limited to known, safe conditions.*
- *Log acknowledgements using system.util.getLogger() if required for auditing.*
- *This logic is best run from a Gateway Timer Script, Alarm Event Script, or Tag Event Script.*

Sample Exercises

Exercise 1: Write to a Tag Based on a Condition

· **Objective**: Turn off a motor if the temperature exceeds 100°F.

Script:

```
temp = system.tag.readBlocking(["[Site A]Boiler/Temp"])[0].value

if temp > 100:
system.tag.writeBlocking(["[Site A]Motor/Enable"], [False])
system.util.getLogger(
                "Automation").info(
                                "Motor disabled due to high temp:
                                " + str(temp)
                                )
```

What You Learn: How to implement conditional tag control using logic and tag writing.

Exercise 2: Reset a Fault Automatically After Delay

· **Objective**: If a device faults, wait 5 seconds and reset it.

Script:

```
def resetFault():
    system.tag.writeBlocking(["[Site A]Pump/FaultReset"], [1])
    system.util.getLogger("Automation").info("Fault reset triggered.")

fault = system.tag.readBlocking(
                        ["[Site A]Pump/Fault"]
                        )[0].value
if fault:
    system.util.invokeLater(resetFault, 5000)
```

What You Learn: How to delay execution with invokeLater() for safe client automation.

Exercise 3: Trigger a Named Query Based on Alarm

- **Objective**: Insert an event into the database when a critical alarm is detected.

Script:

```
alarm = system.tag.readBlocking(["[Site A]Tank/HighLevelAlarm"])[0].value

if alarm:
system.db.runNamedQuery(
                    "InsertEventLog",{
                    "event_type": "HighLevel",
                    "description": "Tank level exceeded"
                    }
                    )
```

What You Learn: How to combine tag logic with named queries for automated logging.

Exercise 4: Send Email on System Condition

· **Objective**: Email maintenance if flow rate drops below threshold.

Script:

```
flow = system.tag.readBlocking(["[Site A]Flow/Rate"])[0].value

if flow < 10:
    body = "Flow rate critically low: " + str(flow)
    system.net.sendEmail(
                    "alerts@yourplant.com",
                    "maintenance@yourplant.com",
                    "Flow Alert",
                    body
                    )
```

What You Learn: How to generate email alerts from script logic tied to live data.

Exercise 5: Batch Control Multiple Devices with a Loop

· **Objective**: Turn off all motors in a group when a stop command is issued.

Script:

```
paths = [
   "[default]Line1/Motor1/Enable",
   "[default]Line1/Motor2/Enable",
   "[default]Line1/Motor3/Enable"
   ]

system.tag.writeBlocking(paths, [False] * len(paths))
print "All motors shut down."
```

What You Learn: How to apply batch control logic across multiple tags.

26

Chapter 26: Debugging and Testing Jython Scripts

Debugging and testing Jython scripts in Ignition is essential for ensuring accuracy and reliability in automation logic. Tools like the Script Console, print statements, and system.util.getLogger() help trace execution and inspect variable values. Proper error handling with try/except blocks aids in identifying and isolating issues. Testing scripts in small sections before full deployment reduces risk and improves maintainability. Mastering debugging techniques leads to cleaner, more robust scripts that perform reliably in live Ignition environments.

26.1 Using the Script Console for Interactive Testing

The **Script Console** in Ignition Designer is your go-to environment for testing Jython code. It's ideal for rapid prototyping, tag manipulation, and debugging without needing to trigger UI events or wait for tag changes.

What You Can Do in the Script Console

Test functions line-by-line

- Quickly validate logic without writing full scripts.

Read and write tags instantly

- Verify tag paths, data types, or simulate values in real time.

Try system functions before deployment

- Experiment with system.tag, system.date, system.db, and more.

Example: Read and Print a Tag Value

```
temp = system.tag.readBlocking(["[Site A]Sensor/Temp"])[0].value
print "Temperature:", temp
```

- Reads the value of [Site A]Sensor/Temp.
- Prints the current temperature to the console output.

Best Practice

Always use the Script Console to test small code blocks before embedding them in:

- *Vision event handlers*
- *Gateway event scripts*
- *Tag change events*
- *Perspective scripts*

This avoids deploying code that may throw errors or cause unexpected behavior.

26.2 Using system.util.getLogger() for Tracing

In Ignition, logging is a critical tool for **understanding script behavior**, **debugging issues**, and **recording runtime events** across Gateway and Client scopes.

Example: Structured Logging with a Named Logger

```
logger = system.util.getLogger("DeviceControl")
logger.info("Start script triggered")
logger.warn("Unexpected input")
logger.error("Write failed")
```

- Creates a logger named "DeviceControl".
- Logs messages at different levels: info, warn, and error.
- Each message appears in the **Gateway Logs** or **Client Diagnostics**, depending on where the script runs.

Why Use Logging

- **Trace script execution** in real time.
- **Identify failure points** (e.g., tag write errors, bad logic).
- **Debug without needing a message box** or UI element.
- **Record user actions** or state changes for auditing.

Best Practices

- *Use clear, consistent logger names like:*
- *"TagLogic" – for tag event scripts*
- *"UserActions" – for button clicks or UI events*
- *"Scheduler" – for Gateway timer tasks*

Use:

- *info() for normal operation*
- *warn() for unexpected but recoverable issues*
- *error() for critical problems that need attention*
- *View logs in the Gateway Web Interface under Status → Logs*

26.3 Handling Exceptions to Expose Errors

Wrapping your scripts in try/except blocks is essential for **error handling** in Ignition. It helps you **prevent script failures**, **log detailed diagnostics**, and **keep systems running smoothly** even when something goes wrong.

Example: Catch and Log a Tag Read Error

FOUNDATIONS OF JYTHON PROGRAMMING

```
try:
  speed = system.tag.readBlocking(
                          ["[Site A]Motors/Motor 1/Speed"]
                          )[0].value
except Exception as e:
  system.util.getLogger("MotorCheck").error("Error reading speed: " + str(e))
```

- Attempts to read the Motors/Motor 1/Speed tag.
- If the tag is missing or misconfigured, the script won't crash — it logs the error instead.
- Uses system.util.getLogger() to trace the error message with context.

Why Use Exception Handling

- **Prevents script failure** in Vision, Perspective, or Gateway scripts.
- **Provides meaningful logs** for developers and operators.
- **Avoids silent failures** that can lead to bad data or system confusion.
- **Improves robustness** of tag events, scheduled tasks, and UI actions.

Best Practices

Always log exceptions with:

The component or tag involved.

- *The full error message using str(e).*
- *Catch Exception to cover most runtime issues unless you expect specific ones (e.g., IOError, ValueError).*

Use consistent logger names (e.g., "AlarmReset", "ReportJob") for easy filtering in logs.

26.4 Structuring Testable Functions

Well-structured scripts improve code quality and project scalability. By breaking logic into small, reusable functions inside **Project Script Modules**, you make it easier to **test, maintain, and reuse** across components and systems.

Example: Create a Helper Function

Inside your Project Library → scripts/helpers.py, define:

```
def isOverLimit(value, limit):
    return value > limit
```

- This simple function checks whether a value exceeds a specified limit.
- It can be reused in tag scripts, UI actions, or reports.

Test It in the Script Console

```
from project.scripts import helpers
print helpers.isOverLimit(90, 75) # Output: True
```

- Quickly verify function behavior without UI interaction.
- Confirms the logic is sound before embedding in production scripts.

Why Modular Functions Matter

- *Improve readability by isolating business logic from event handlers.*
- *Simplify testing using the Script Console.*
- *Enable reuse across buttons, timers, tags, and reports.*
- *Support versioning and upgrades by modifying logic in one place.*

26.5 Best Practices for Debugging in Ignition

Effective debugging is essential for building reliable automation and SCADA applications in Ignition. Use these practices to detect issues early and validate script behavior across environments.

Core Debugging Tips

Use the Script Console for all new logic

- Test functions, tag reads/writes, and dataset logic interactively before deployment.

Log before and after key operations

- Insert logging statements to trace script flow, variable values, and conditional paths.

Create test tags and test windows

- Use sandbox environments to safely prototype without affecting production.

Use print in the Script Console

- Ideal for quick testing and variable inspection during development.

Use system.util.getLogger() in production

- Provides structured logging with levels (info, warn, error) and supports filtering in Gateway logs.

Always test with both expected and unexpected inputs

- Include nulls, out-of-range values, bad types, and disconnected tags to ensure resilience.

USe the Vision Client Diagnostics Console

Enable with Ctrl+Shift+F7 (in Vision Client).

View:

- *Script execution*
- *Memory usage*
- *Thread activity*
- *Component updates*

Helps you identify performance bottlenecks, errors, and slow-running scripts.

Sample Exercises

Exercise 1: Use the Script Console for Iterative Testing

· **Objective**: Manually test tag reads and logic using the built-in Script Console.

Script (in Tools > Script Console):

```
val = system.tag.readBlocking(["[Site A]Motors/Motor 1/Speed"])[0].value
print "Pump speed =", val
```

What You Learn: How to test individual lines or blocks of code quickly in isolation.

Exercise 2: Use system.util.getLogger() for Custom Logging

· **Objective**: Log debugging info during script execution.

Script:

```
logger = system.util.getLogger("DebugPump")
speed = system.tag.readBlocking(["[Site A]Motors/Motor 1/Speed)[0].value

logger.info("Read speed: " + str(speed))
if speed > 1500:
logger.warn("Speed is above normal!")
```

What You Learn: How to insert meaningful logs into scripts and check output in the Logs tab.

Exercise 3: Isolate Errors with Try/Except Blocks

- **Objective**: Prevent scripts from failing silently and catch issues clearly.

Script:

```
try:
    pressure = system.tag.readBlocking(["[default]Boiler/Pressure"])[0].value
    print "Pressure =", pressure
except Exception as e:
    system.util.getLogger(
                "DebugBoiler").error("Failed to read pressure: " +    str(e)
                )
```

What You Learn: How to use exception handling to capture and trace runtime errors.

Exercise 4: Test Script Logic with Dummy Data

- **Objective**: Create test functions with hardcoded values before going live with tags.

Script:

FOUNDATIONS OF JYTHON PROGRAMMING

```
def testFlowLogic(flow):
    if flow < 5:
        return "ALERT: Flow too low!"
    return "Flow is acceptable."

# Run with test data
print testFlowLogic(3.2)
print testFlowLogic(7.5)
```

What You Learn: How to write unit-style functions and test them with sample input.

Exercise 5: Verify Named Query Behavior with Print Debugging

- **Objective**: Confirm what data is returned from a named query.

Script:

```
results = system.db.runNamedQuery("GetDeviceList", {}, "MyDB")
pyData = system.dataset.toPyDataSet(results)

for row in pyData:
    print "Device:", row["name"], "| Status:", row["status"]
```

What You Learn: How to confirm query results before applying automation logic.

Appendix A: Java Quick Reference

How to Import Java Classes

Basic syntax:

- **from java.package import ClassName**

Example:

- **from java.util import Date**

Common Java Packages You Will Use

- java.util → Dates, Collections (like lists and maps)
- java.lang → Math functions, system info, basic utilities
- java.text → Date and time formatting
- javax.crypto → Encryption (advanced topics)

Useful Java Classes for HMI/SCADA Scripting

Date and Time

Current date and time:

```
from java.util import Date
now = Date()
```

Custom date formatting:

```
from java.text import SimpleDateFormat
formatter = SimpleDateFormat("yyyy-MM-dd HH:mm:ss")
print formatter.format(Date())
```

Precise system timestamp (milliseconds):

```
from java.lang import System
print System.currentTimeMillis()
```

Math Operations

Advanced math functions:

```
from java.lang import Math
print Math.sqrt(144)    # Square root
print Math.pow(2, 8)    # 2 to the power of 8
print Math.abs(-15)     # Absolute value
```

Lists and Maps

Dynamic list (like Python list):

```
from java.util import ArrayList
devices = ArrayList()
devices.add("Motor")
devices.add("Valve")
print devices
```

Dynamic key-value map (like Python dictionary):

```
from java.util import HashMap
settings = HashMap()
settings.put("Speed", 100)
settings.put("Temperature", 250)
print settings
```

System Information

Retrieve system properties:

```
from java.lang import System
print System.getProperty("os.name")     # Operating System
print System.getProperty("user.name")   # Current user
print System.getProperty("java.version") # Java version
```

◆ Common Real-World Uses

Task	Java Class to Import	Example
Format a custom timestamp	SimpleDateFormat	Format alarms or log timestamps
Measure how long a device runs	System.currentTimeMillis()	Calculate elapsed time
Create a dynamic device list	ArrayList	Track motors, valves, sensors
Store device settings	HashMap	Speed, pressure, temperature values
Display client system info	System.getProperty()	Diagnostics or audit screens